WALKING

A daily meditation book about recovery, based on the Bible.

Written by Andrea Lynn Bowman
Inspired by Jesus Christ
Dedicated to prisoners of any addiction everywhere

About the Author

My name is Andrea Bowman. I've lived a life like many others; perhaps, a life similar to yours. In my sane and sober moments, I wanted to change my life but didn't have the strength to do it. I realized I had lost my self respect, forsaken my children, alienated my family, and was slowly killing myself. My life progressed from bad to worse. I looked in the mirror and saw a stranger-one I did not like. Perhaps, you see the same.

My main desire in writing my story and my steps of recovery down on paper is the hope that it will lead others to Christ and give God the glory He is due for changing my life. God has restored my self-esteem, my family relationships, my daughters, my health, and given me unconditional love, peace, joy, acceptance, and forgiveness.

I am including a brief "picture" of my past in the hope that some of my readers will recognize themselves and realize that no matter where they are in their life, they still have a choice to change because nothing is impossible for God (Mark 10:27).

It all started when I ran away from home at 14 years old. Not wanting to abide by my parents rules, I decided to go out on my own. I hitchhiked to San Francisco where I knew no one. I found myself living on the streets resorting to prostitution and theft to support myself.

Within a very short period of time, I became involved in drugs so deeply that without them I became physically sick. I resorted to any means I could to support my habits. Throughout the years I went to several treatment facilities and attended different recovery programs. These only helped for short periods of time before they failed and I returned back to my old habits.

I became involved in many unhealthy and violent relationships during my addiction including numerous failed marriages. I subjected my children to severe emotional upheaval which led me to losing my parental rights and my daughters being taken away.

In the midst of my fast-lane living, I was exposed to Hepatitis C and HIV along with my drug use. I became very sick and, at one point, several doctors told me I had less than 6 months to live.

This only drove me further from my family and deeper into my addiction. I had lost hope in my life and felt that I deserved whatever happened to me. At one point, I was arrested and jailed but the amount of time I spent locked down was not sufficient enough for the fog to lift and my thinking to clear.

Once back on the street, I started manufacturing my own drugs. This time out, I was worse off that before – running rampant in vicious circles of addiction until I was finally arrested again in 2005. This time I received a sentence of 8 years. Four years to be served in the Washington Corrections Center for Women and four years of strict parole.

During my incarceration, I began to read my Bible and go to church. While attending chapel in the prison, I met a woman named Pastor Jody Pickney who took an interest in my spiritual well being. It was because of her encouragement and the godly example she set for all of the women prisoners in her services that my outlook began to change. I started on a new path to recovery.

From the beginning of this journey, I have discovered the love of my life, Jesus Christ, and He has set me free from the bondage of addiction, sin, and death. My inspiration is Jesus, and through His power and the Holy Spirit, this book was made possible.

My qualifications for writing this book are based on my life experiences and my faith in Christ to guide my pen. My task is not to convince you of God's grace and wisdom in my own words, but to testify of the truth of the gospel and God's love for each of us individually.

In our own way, we are all prisoners to something or someone. Why not be set free by Christ Jesus? The end result will give you strength for the present, hope for the future and peace for eternity. I hope this book will bless you, inspire you, and influence your heart, mind, and soul. Change is possible —I am living proof! God bless you.

Sincerely, Andrea L. Bowman

DELIVERANCE

In my darkest, coldest hour when things were looking bleak,
I found myself upon the ground, my face at Jesus' feet.
"Rise up, my child," He kindly said, "you're forgiven, you're healed, you're free.
I've paid the price. I've borne your pain. Just put your faith in Me.
Don't look upon your circumstances as appearances can be deceiving,
Put your faith in My love for you then My blessings you'll start receiving.
I've given you the ears to hear and the eyes to see,
Just open up your heart my child, and put your faith in Me."

FOREWORD

When you think of Christ, what picture do you perceive? A Savior who longs to wrap Himself around every part of your life and being, surrounding you with love, or a distant judgmental entity shaking his head in disapproval at the human race?

The Bible says God loves us and that "<u>God is love</u>."

I John 4:8-10
"He who does not love does not know God, for God is love. In this the love of God was manifested toward us, that God has sent His only begotten Son into the world, that we might live through Him. In this is love, not that we loved God, but that He loved us and sent His Son to be the propitiation (full payment) for our sins."

I John 4:18-19
"There is no fear in love; but perfect love casts out fear, because fear involves torment. But he who fears has not been made perfect in love. We love Him because He first loved us."

God's love is perfect! His love does not judge but protects and strengthens. God's love never fails!

> Consultation with God brings revelation which leads to transformation that brings restoration. Amen

CONTENTS

Introduction / About the Author
Foreword
Day 1   Addiction
Day 2   Road of Life
Day 3   Anger Management
Day 4   Commitment and Prayer
Day 5   Serenity
Day 6   Fear in Addiction
Day 7   God's Love
Day 8   Disguised Blessings
Day 9   Reflections
Day 10   The Cheater
Day 11   Forgiveness
Day 12   Hope
Day 13   Faith
Day 14   Healing and Restoration
Day 15   Fellowship
Day 16   Choices
Day 17   Joy
Day 18   A Humbling Experience
Day 19   Important Relationships
Day 20   Sowing and Reaping
Day 21   Salvation, the Free Gift
Day 22   From Desire to Destiny
Day 23   Adversities
Day 24   Sin in Our Lives
Day 25   The Witness
Day 26   Down Time
Day 27   Honesty
Day 28   Thankfulness
Day 29   Worship
Day 30   The Love of Money
Day 31   God's Guarantee
Day 32   Who is God?

Day 33	Wisdom
Day 34	Letting Go of the "What Ifs"
Day 35	From Where Does My Help Come?
Day 36	Sharing the Burden
Day 37	A Heart Dedicated
Day 38	The Bible Our Foundation
Day 39	Tools of the Trade
Day 40	Walking in the Spirit

Closing Thoughts

Day 1

"ADDICTION"

Matthew 19:26
"...With men this is impossible, but with God all things are possible."

The difference between stumbling blocks and stepping stones is how you use them. Is your cup half empty or half full?

The way we live depends on how we view things in our lives. The way we view things depends upon our belief systems. Optimism and pessimism are the two roads we travel in life. The road you choose to travel is up to you. However, I believe anyone can change their future by changing their views. If you keep your eyes on Christ, and your hope in His Word, anything is possible. Change in our lives comes as a result of having our mind renewed by God's Word.

As we study God's Word and learn about His will for us, it will gradually start to manifest itself in us. Eventually, what we put in our hearts will be seen on the outside.

By filling our heart and mind with God's Word, we will change - having new attitudes, good habits, good health, and an all around godly life style.

Any addiction can be overcome with Christ in your life. Have you ever seen a dog chasing its tail? We consider this a funny sight, yes? Well in comparison to how we act as addicts, we are no different from that dog. It isn't that we're chasing anything in particular - just running in circles not even aware of how foolish we look.

Proverbs 19:3
"The foolishness of a man twists his way, And his heart frets against the Lord."

How true this is for us in addiction. Our own foolishness leads us down so many paths to destruction...destruction of our families, homes, physical health, and even our emotional health. As we chase our "tails" in addiction, running in circles of unhappiness, we wear ourselves down chasing drugs, alcohol, sex, money, and many other things finding no complete satisfaction.

As I look back in my mind's eye and think about the dog chasing his tail, I see a reflection of my own behavior If you grab his tail so he can catch it, what does the dog do? He stops only momentarily to chew himself and then wiggles out of your grasp to resume the chase. As addicts, our relationships with God, family, and friends is similar. Every time they try to get our attention we don't really stop long enough to listen or stop running in those vicious circles of addition.

Proverbs 23:9
"Do not speak the hearing of a fool, For he will despise the wisdom of your words."
When my family and friends tried to break through to me, I heard nothing. Unfortunately, as addicts many of us have to experience the wrath of our own bad decisions before we get tired of running in those circles.

In my case, those bad decisions included consuming drugs and manufacturing methamphetamine. My manufacturing led to a higher consumption of drugs causing immoral behavior and a lust for money and material things.

Those worldly desires led me deeper into the drug world to fulfill all of my so called "needs", which landed me in prison. Now in recovery, Alcohol Anonymous (AA), Narcotics Anonymous (NA), and the Bible say addiction leads only three places—jails, institutions, and death.

As I sat there and did my prison time, God finally had my full attention. I know now that God's Word and the knowledge that it holds can and will help me recover and live a spirit filled life in recovery. It's like I said earlier in the chapter, there are two roads in life with two final destinations. Each of us must choose the path we wish to follow.

Today I choose the high road which leads to life through Christ, and in Him, I pray we all choose to dwell. The low road is the way of the wicked, the flesh, and the desires for worldly things. The low road is a bad choice because God says "the way of the wicked vanishes."

Proverbs 13:13
"He who despises the word will be destroyed, But he who fears the commandment will be rewarded."

Proverbs 14:9
"Fools mock at sin, But among the upright there is favor"

At this point, I would like to say if you are serious about recovery based on God's Word, I urge you to continue reading and my prayer for you is that the blessings of the Lord will be upon you as they have been upon me.

Prayer:

Father God, we praise You now for our free will. To be able to make our own choices is truly a gift. I pray, Lord, for your guidance and wisdom to make right choices in life and to follow the right path. Help me, Lord Jesus, to keep my eyes on You and to never stray from the high road. Amen

Day 2

"ROAD OF LIFE"

Psalm 1:6
"For the Lord knows the way of the righteous, But the way of the ungodly shall perish."

The road of life is very short and completely unpredictable. You should never plan too far ahead. Many times when we do, we end up out of God's will. Learning to trust Him on a day-to-day basis is very important. When you get ahead of God and His will for you, it can be very overwhelming. "One day at a time" is one of my favorite mottos that we should all try to apply to our lives. Learning not to over-do it and overwhelm ourselves with our daily lives is a tough job for an addict, even in recovery - especially some one like me who has a terrible habit of doing everything in excess.

Slowly, I'm learning that my "higher power" (God) has to be my focal point at all times. When I start to get into my needs, and my wants, and my desires, not focusing on God's will and His Word, I stumble. It is at these different mile markers in my life that I must stop to re-evaluate and refocus on what the Lord expects of me.

When I take time out to reconnect with my "higher power" (God) through prayer and by meditating on what the Bible says about whatever I'm going through is when I can truly recognize that small, still voice that is the Holy Spirit. The key from there is following those whisperings and nudging of the Spirit. Remember God speaks through His Word, therefore, you must be diligent in reading the Bible and referring to it for advice.

If you really want to change your life circumstances, let God "drive the car" for awhile. Rémember "one day at a time"; include God in your daily life and your entire decision making. Do your best to abide in His commandments on a daily basis. I know one thing for sure – life's journey is much more pleasurable and beautiful than I ever imagined with Jesus at the wheel. I've finally learned that His will for me is actually my will in the long run. I truly believe Jesus just wants us to relax, enjoy this ride called life, and let Him drive.

Matthew 11:28-30
"Come unto Me, all you who labor and are heavy laden, and I will give you rest. Take My yoke upon you and learn from Me, for I am gentle and lowly in heart, and you will find rest for your souls. For My yoke is easy and My burden is light."

Thank God that He is willing to take responsibility if we will let Him in, only giving us what we can endure a little at a time.

Isaiah 58: 11
"The Lord will guide you continually, and satisfy your soul in drought, and strengthen your bones; You shall be like a watered garden, And like a spring of water, whose waters do not fail."

What this is saying to us is that even in our most lonely, awkward, confusing times (our parched places) that we are not alone. God is always there waiting for us to seek His help. As we learn to depend on God's strength in our weakness, He helps us to learn from our trials. We must remember that on the other side of those trials, we will be "like a watered garden, like a spring of water whose waters never will fail" if we rely on Him.

God wants us to be present and aware of where we are in life. He wants us to see, hear, and feel what is around us. Hopefully, this way we will learn to lean on Him in time of need instead of trying to solve everything on our own. God wants to be included in your life, every aspect of it. Let us open our eyes to His love and our ears to the wisdom of His Word.

"HELP ME"

Help me to be holy, Lord, to hear your call upon my life,
Put a bridle in my mouth, oh Lord, that I may generate no strife.
Take the scales from my eyes that I can clearly see,
Show me what it is, oh Lord, that you expect from me.
Cast down Satan's thoughts and lies; clean them from my mind,
Create in me a clean heart, Lord, and in me no sin find.
I truly want to do what's right and not what's wrong,
I truly need your might and strength to carry me along.
Without You, I am small and weak and darkness fills my soul,
I need Your joy, love and light to make me feel whole.
"Help me Holy Father" is my cry to you,
You're all I ever need or want in life to make it through.
To make it through all life's trials and to the other side,
Lord with you, I hide my heart, in you, Lord, I abide.

John 16:33
"These things I have spoken to you, that in Me you may have peace. In the world you will have tribulation; but be of good cheer, I have overcome the world."

All in all we really have no worries when we rely on Him and His promise.

So on that note, my friends, remember don't live your life like a flickering candle. Live your life blazing like the sun. Let your life shine with significance. Let your life reflect God's glory moment to moment. Let every purpose you fulfill reflect love, for to love is the greatest of all commandments. Let the love you share with others reflect Christ every day that you live.

Prayer:
Father, help me to view myself and my situation through your eyes. Let the love of Christ be seen in my life daily. Amen

Day 3

"ANGER MANAGEMENT"

Psalm 37:8
"Cease from anger, and forsake wrath; Do not fret – it only causes harm."

Ephesians 4:26-27
"Be angry, and do not sin: do not let the sun go down on your wrath, nor give place to the devil."

I know when I read this for the first time my thought was "is anger a sin?" I don't believe so but how you deal with it can be. I believe to act on anger is a sin. When we dwell on angry thoughts, our thoughts become actions and those actions can be sinful.

The Bible tells us in Ephesians 4:31-32, *"Let all bitterness, wrath, anger, clamor, and evil speaking be put away from you, with all malice. And be kind to one another, tender- hearted, forgiving one another, even as God in Christ forgave you."*

Showing mercy to our fellow man can be a difficult task to perform, especially when we feel like we've been wronged by the other party involved.

I know that many times in my life I've had a very difficult time letting go of grudges. Over time I am learning that when I don't show mercy to others and forgive them, I start to build up animosity toward that party or situation. My thought patterns toward anyone involved become vindictive and revengeful. At this point it's time to stop and call upon my "higher power" (Jesus) and His Word. If I don't, my thoughts can become actions, leaving the devil joyous, while I am still angry and hurt. The good news is if I do choose to call upon Jesus, I can avoid the whole negative pattern I just described. In the New Testament, Jesus tells us to follow in His footsteps and to walk His path. In doing so, we should always show mercy to others.

Psalm 103:8 states, *"The Lord is merciful and gracious, Slow to anger, and abounding in mercy."*

Psalm 86:15
"But You, O Lord, are a God full of compassion, and gracious, Long suffering and abundant in mercy and truth."

Now I remember in my addiction when I was using, I had a tendency to have a short fuse and to "fly off the handle", overreacting in almost all situations. But in recovery when I walk in God's Word, I find I have more control over my thought patterns, attitudes, and actions. On the occasion when I do "fly off the handle", I simply cry out to Jesus to help me like David did in Psalm 51:1, *"Have mercy upon me, O God, according to Your loving kindness; According to the multitude of Your tender mercies, Blot out my transgressions."*

So my friends, when you have an issue with some one or some thing, reflect on God's mercy and love toward us before reacting and ask yourself, "What would Jesus do?"

Romans 12:10-12
"Be kindly and affectionate one to another with brotherly love, in honor giving preference to one another; not lagging in diligence, fervent in spirit, serving the Lord; rejoicing in hope, patient in tribulation, continuing steadfastly in prayer;"

Prayer:
Lord Jesus, thank You for your loyalty to me as my Savior, my brother, my confident and my friend. Thank you for your mercy, forgiveness and grace. I pray, through the empowerment of the Holy Spirit, I can learn to be more like You. Help me to be tender-hearted and to forgive others showing them the same mercy and grace You show me. Open my heart to see others through Your eyes. Amen

Day 4

"COMMITMENT AND PRAYER"

Psalm 37:5
"Commit your way to the Lord, Trust also in Him, And He shall bring it to pass."

Surrender to God daily and ask Him for His help and guidance – this is the best advice I've ever gotten from anyone. Many times in life when we encounter situations we fear, we panic. How often we slip and forget that, as a Christian, we have committed our way to God. When this happens we must take a step back and reapply this verse to our lives: *"Commit your way to the Lord,"* then remind ourselves, *"trust in Him."* As believers we must learn to surrender every area of our lives to His wise control on a daily basis. I cannot stress enough how important this is. Surrendering in prayer to God's will is the best bridge between panic and peace. When we start our day with Jesus, it helps us throughout our whole day. As natural born sinners, we all need constant reminding of what God expects of us. I know when I start my day with prayer I gather peace of mind and strength of heart, leaving me more open to hear God's voice when He speaks to me.

Jesus, our Great Intercessor to God the Father, tells us He pleads on our behalf for us.

It says in Psalm 34:15-17, *"The eyes of the Lord are on the righteous, And His ears are open to their cry. The face of the Lord is against those who do evil, To cut off remembrance of them from the earth. The righteous cry out, and the Lord hears, And delivers them out of all their troubles."*

The Lord is always listening; His desire is for us to call on Him not just in times of trouble but at all times. Conversing with God should not feel like a burden or something that is expected of you. Sharing time with the Lord should be a joy.

God does not judge us on how we pray. He just wants to hear from us on a consistent basis. We must remember God knows everything about us - every action, every thought.
The Lord wants to extend his love to every individual in all areas of their life.

Matthew 7:7
"Ask, and it will be given to you; seek, and you will find; knock, and it will be opened to you."

In order for these things to come to pass, we must ask God for His help. God is not intrusive. We must give ourselves and our will over to Him daily through prayer and meditation.

In Psalm 143:8 the psalmist cries out to the Lord in the same way He longs to hear from
us: *"Cause me to hear Your loving kindness in the morning, For in You I do trust; Cause me to know the way in which I should walk, For I lift up my soul to You."*

I can honestly say I am still learning about what God expects of me and to pay attention to my actions and thoughts every moment. It is important that we daily empty ourselves of "self" so that God can occupy a larger space in our lives. The more I pray and talk to Him, the closer I feel drawn to His majestic grace and everlasting love. No one in this life time can ever love us the way Jesus does. The reflection of His life in the New Testament and how He lived, died, and rose again proves that. My prayer for you is that you seek Him and ask Him to be a part of your life. God loves you and accepts you just as you are! He wants a personal relationship with you.

John 3:16-17
"For God so loved the world that He gave His only begotten Son, that whoever believes in Him should not perish but have everlasting life. For God did not send His Son into the world to condemn the world, but that the world through Him might be saved."

It's so simple to make God a part of your life. If you don't know how, just pray and say, "Lord Jesus, I want and need you in my life. I now accept you as my personal Savior. Lord, help me to grow in You. Amen"

The Bible says in I John 5:11-12, *"And this is the testimony: that God has given us eternal life, and this life is in His Son. He who has the Son has life; he who does not have the Son of God does not have life."* Jesus is the answer in this life and in the next! You can trust in God, and in His love for you!

My friends, let Jesus open your heart and enlighten your mind for all things are possible with God. In Psalm 91:14-15, the Bible tells us, *"Because he has set his love upon Me, therefore I will deliver him; I will set him on high, because he has known My name. He shall call upon Me, and I will answer him; I will be with him in trouble; I will deliver him and honor him."*

Here are four important steps to help you find and know God, to help you love and accept yourself, and to help you grow in faith and live a Christian life. These steps may not always be easy to do but are vital to your success in life and in recovery.
1. Set aside time each day to read and meditate on God's Word.
2. Find a quiet place to reflect and pray, concentrate on Him alone during this time.
3. Seek Him daily applying His Word to <u>all</u> situations in your life.

4. Remember nothing is too big or too small for God to accomplish.

Matthew 6:6
"But you, when you pray, go into your room, and when you have shut your door, pray to your Father who is in the secret place; and your Father who sees in secret will reward you openly."

James 5:13
"Is anyone among you suffering? Let him pray."

Jeremiah 29:12-13
Then you will call upon Me and go and pray to Me, and I will listen to you. And you will seek Me and find Me, when you search for Me with all your heart."

ONLY PLEASING YOU

Only pleasing You, Lord, is truly my life's goal,
To you I open my heart and mind and dedicate my soul.
An indwelling of Your Spirit will surely renew my mind,
Washing away the sins of the past and leaving them all behind.
To refresh and renew the inner man is the promise you've made to me,
By opening up my life to You, You promise to set me free.
I give You all my burdens, my sorrows, and my loss,
As my Father, You smile and say, "Leave them at the cross.
I give you love and healing and forgiveness through my Son,
Open up your heart to me and we shall be as one."

Prayer:
> Heavenly Father, please help me to relinquish myself to You and Your will for me. Lord take my life and make it Yours; I trust You. I now commit every aspect of my life to You - my will, my passion, myself and my pride. I now surrender Lord, in me abide. Amen

Day 5

"SERENITY"

John 14:27
"Peace I leave with you, My peace I give to you; not as the world gives do I give to you. Let not your heart be troubled, neither let it be afraid."

As I work daily on my recovery keeping God as my focus, I am finding that the thing I strive for most is serenity. I truly believe as human beings we are all in a daily struggle to achieve this major goal – to be at peace in our lives.

I, personally, as a Christian in recovery, pray continually all through the day for God's help, advice, strength, and for His will, not my own, to be in control of my desires.

When I first quit using drugs, one of those prayers often included the "Serenity Prayer" by Reinhold Niebuhr. The first verse is often used by AA. "God, grant me the serenity to accept the things I cannot change, courage to change the things I can, and the wisdom to know the difference."

When I began to really meditate on this prayer, I began to contemplate its meaning. I've found it falls into three requests for help from our Heavenly Father: acceptance, courage, and wisdom. Now I prayed this prayer many, many times before I really meant it. When this finally happened, God opened my eyes to see that my only success in achieving any of these three things were going to be through Him and His Word. What many people don't realize is God has given us the answers we already seek for acceptance, courage, and wisdom.

Acceptance: It brings about forgiveness, mercy and grace. Psalm 107:17-20 says, *"Fools, because of their transgression, And because of their iniquities, were afflicted. …and they drew near to the gates of death. Then they cried out to the Lord in their trouble, And He saved them out of their distresses. He sent His word and healed them, And delivered them from their destructions."* When we accept that we need God's help and call on Him, He will answer!

Courage: Find courage and strength in God's promises.

Psalm 103:2-4
"Bless the Lord, O my soul, And forget not all His benefits: Who forgives all your iniquities (sins), Who heals all your diseases, Who redeems your life from destruction, Who crowns you with loving kindness and tender mercies."

I John 5:4-5
"For whatever is born of God overcomes the world. And this is the victory that has overcome the world-our faith. Who is he who overcomes the world, but he who believes that Jesus is the Son of God?"

Philippians 4:13
"I can do all things through Christ who strengthens me."

With Jesus all things are possible. He is our strength; therefore, we should be courageous.

Wisdom: The Word of God is wisdom and all the knowledge we need to live by.

Proverbs 2:10-11
"When wisdom enters your heart, and knowledge is pleasant to your soul, Discretion will preserve you; Understanding will keep you."

Romans 8:3-6

"For what the law could not do in that it was weak through the flesh, God did by sending His own Son in the likeness of sinful flesh, on account of sin: He condemned sin in the flesh, that the righteous requirement of the law might be fulfilled in us who do not walk according to the flesh but according to the Spirit. For those who live according to the flesh set their minds on the things of the flesh, but those who live according to the Spirit, the things of the Spirit. For to be carnally minded is death, but to be spiritually minded is life and peace."

Life and peace! Looking back at those verses, we can plainly see that God has made it clear in His Word that all of these things – life, peace, and serenity – are ours if we seek Him. The fact that He loves us all so much is almost too overwhelming to believe, but He does!

I can honestly say I have found serenity and peace of mind for my soul in God's Word and in my faith in Christ. So can you if you choose to.

Prayer:
>Lord Jesus, today I seek your guidance. Lord, I want perfect peace which only comes from You. Help me to follow the path which You have planned for me that I may know the true meaning of serenity in my life.
>Amen

Day 6

"FEAR IN ADDICTION"

Isaiah 12:2
"God is my salvation, I will trust and not be afraid."

Fear is one of the most dangerous emotions we deal with. Fear is one of the devil's favorite tools to use to clutter our minds and confuse us. More frequently than not, fear pushes us into actions that draw us away from God.

Actively using addicts fear many things which drive them to try and deaden these emotions with the use of mind altering chemicals. Drug use then leads to more shame and guilt for our behavior, causing us to run further from our families, friends, and God and His grace. We must learn to halt this process before it starts.

We must learn to look to Jesus for power, strength, and love. II Timothy 1:7 says, *"God does not give us the spirit of fear but of power and of love and of a sound mind."* We need to remember God is all powerful. We have nothing to fear if we let Him control our lives and let go of our own stubborn will. After all, He promises in His Word to instruct us, guide us, and light our path at all times. We must learn to trust God in spite of our circumstances and not be afraid.

Psalm 32:8
"I will instruct you and teach you in the way you should go; I will guide you with My eye."

Proverbs 3:5-6

"Trust in the Lord with all your heart, And lean not on your own understanding; In all your ways acknowledge Him, and He shall direct your paths."

Deuteronomy 31:8
"And the Lord, He is the One who goes before you. He will be with you, He will not leave you nor forsake you; do not fear nor be dismayed."

Even when we are afraid, as Christians, we must remember that God is always by our side. All we need to do is call on Him, and He will answer us. We may not always like the answer we are given; but as our Father, He always has our best interest at heart.

As addicts most of us form habits of running from God and not to Him because we think we know what's best for us. Oh how untrue this is! In reality our will self destructs 100% of the time. Fear of what others may think of us or what God thinks about our actions can cause a chain reaction pushing us toward more negative behavior such as running away from those we love and God. Guilt about our addiction leads to fear as well, drawing us even further down the wrong path and away from God and family.

A simple solution to still this fear is to stay in the Word, reading and praying every day. Stay within the Lord's boundaries, my friends, and He will guide you and strengthen you - I promise! I am a walking, talking example of His grace in action. Recovery based on the Word works. To anyone out there still lost and afraid and living in the nightmare of addiction, don't give in to the "spirit of fear." Instead try the simple solution of reading God's instruction for your life, and He will conquer all of your demons for you. Be careful, though, to remember we are human and easily can go astray and fall back into our old patterns and behaviors if we don't focus on God alone to help us change.

Jesus tells us in the New Testament in Luke 11:24-26, *"When an unclean spirit goes out of a man, he goes through many dry places, seeking rest, and finding none, he says, 'I will return to the house from which I came.' And when he comes, he finds it swept and clean, put in order. Then he goes and takes with him seven other spirits more wicked than himself, and they enter and dwell there, and the last state of the man is worse that the first."*

In AA and NA, addicts talk about relapse and how it's always much worse than the first time they dealt with their addiction. To avoid this situation, we need a new beginning – a fresh start. Being "born again" in Christ (totally giving ourselves to Him), we must break old habits and routines, changing everything about ourselves. This change includes interaction with negative people, places, and things…leaving behind the old man and the past. By doing this, we will conquer the "spirit of fear" in Jesus' name by being renewed in our minds and hearts through Christ for in Him is victory.

Exodus 33:14
"My presence will go with you, and I will give you rest."

Prayer:

Lord, we come to you now with a grateful heart and an uplifted spirit. We praise You for victory over the "spirit of fear." We thank you for the strength You give us daily to endure life's problems. We thank You for Your everlasting love. Amen

Day 7

"GOD'S LOVE"

John 3:16
"For God so loved the world that He gave His only begotten Son, that whoever believes in Him shall not perish but have everlasting life."

Have you ever wondered, "How important is God's love?" Well, without it we are eternally doomed. Have you ever said, "What has He ever done for me?" The first thing that comes to my mind is Jesus' death and resurrection. He loved us enough to send His only Son.

Now as a mother of two girls, I can't even fathom the anguish I would go through if I lost one of my daughters. But God and His love for us is so overpowering that there was no hesitation on His part, not to lose, but to give up His child to reconcile all of us to Himself.

To me, that's deep, but it doesn't end there. Jesus, being part of the Trinity of God (the Son), came to earth to be a sacrifice; God incarnate literally gives His life. Is that not love? He suffered greatly and was killed by human hands so that we could accept God's gift of salvation. How precious a gift can one give? Jesus loves us so much He was willing to die for us just like it says in the Bible.

John 15:13
"Greater love has no one than this, than to lay down one's life for his friends."

No one loves us more than our Savior He reassures us of this in Romans 8:38-39: *"For I am persuaded that neither death nor life, nor angels nor principalities nor powers, nor things present nor things to come, nor height nor depth, nor any other created thing, shall be able to separate us from the love of God which is in Christ Jesus our Lord."*

Let's really mull this over for a minute. Can you imagine losing a child? Can you picture giving <u>your</u> child up in order to save all others for eternity? That, my friends is immeasurable love. I know all my life all I ever wanted was someone to love me. Guess what? Someone does!

GOD'S LOVE

Your mercy and goodness are unbelievable,
Your long suffering, patience, and forgiveness unfathomable,
Your love is immeasurable,
You alone are King of Kings, Lord of Lords,
And the name above all names,
You are the great "I AM."
The concept of your glorious majesty is beyond my mind's boundaries,
The thought of being in your presence overwhelms me and I weep,
I compare your love for me to the depth of the ocean,
And to the boundaries of the universe – there is no comparison!
You, Lord, fill my every need for survival; You are my perfect love,
You alone have shown me every consideration in your life, death, and resurrection.
You are my comforter, my healer, my strength, my protection, my guidance,
   my love and my life.

As Your daughter, I wonder, "Am I worthy?" and I cry out to You.
Your response, "Why are you weeping, My child. You are forgiven,
   you are healed, you are loved, and you are Mine!
Rise up and be strengthened that your joy may be full.
You are where I want you to be when you abide in Me.
Be still and know that I am God and I love you."

Prayer
Lord, we praise You and thank You for Your concern and care for us. I pray that when I have doubt, I will think of Christ's sacrifice for me. We praise You, Father, for Your immeasurable love, unfathomable grace, and for salvation eternal through You. Amen

Day 8

"DISGUISED BLESSINGS"

Genesis 28:15
"Behold, I am with you, I will keep you wherever you go…"

Sometimes in our addiction, we do crazy things we wouldn't normally do; things that get us into extreme amounts of trouble. When I look back at some of the places I've been and situations I put myself in, I wonder, "How did I ever make it through?"

Jesus had to have been with me the whole time, or I would not have survived. When I look at some of the choices I made in my addiction, I realize my idea of what's good for me and my will for what I want is dangerous. Luckily for me, God's will prevailed.

God protects us and blesses us continually by showing us mercy and grace even when we don't give Him credit for it. I cannot count how many times God has turned bad into good in my life. When He does these things, I call them "disguised blessings."

Prison for me was a disguised blessing. Now some people may not see it that way, but for me it was a "time out" so that God could help me refocus on what was truly important in my life. It was a time of healing in my body and a time of reflection on my behaviour and how it affected all the people in my life that love me. It helped me to realize how important freedom really is.

Some of the bad experiences I had while living on the street (like abusing drugs), God has used to teach me how to be more kind, considerate, and open to others' needs. For example, when I found out my daughter was experimenting with drugs; it gave me a better understanding of how she was feeling. This helped me to be more patient and compassionate toward her needs. My experiences turned out to be a blessing in disguise. God says in His Word that all things work out for the good of those who love Him. (Romans 8:28) No matter what you are going through always look for a "silver-lining."

Learning to praise God in all situations can be difficult, but we must remember that God needs to be the one in control concerning us. When you look at all the trials you've been through, or may be facing now, try to view them from a different perspective. How many "disguised blessings" can you count in your life? Make a list, you might be surprised at God's grace in action in your life and you didn't even know it.

For so many years, I couldn't resist the temptation of a very sinful life style. Between drug use, prostitution, manufacturing drugs, stealing and lying, I was drowning in a sea of iniquity (sin) and guilt. Thanks be to God that He picked me up out of the nasty web I'd woven.

In recovery, I have found that every trial I've faced, God has used to enable me to help others and myself. Through Christ, my life has become successful and productive. I want to give God glory for shaping me slowly into a better daughter, friend, and mother. He can do the same for you.

HE'S THE ONE

He's the One to call on when life's problems get you down,

He's the One to call on when there's no one else around.
He's the only One I know who turns darkness into light,
My redeemer is the only One who changes wrong into right.

Jeremiah 33:3
"Call to Me, and I will answer you, and show you great and mighty things, which you do not know."

Prayer:
Dear Lord, help me to keep my eyes on You at all times. Let me be in Your will daily, Lord. Let my actions follow Your voice and not the pressures of the world or other people. Help me, Father, to conduct myself in a manner worthy of You, fully trying to please You in all things. Amen

Day 9

"REFLECTIONS"

Psalm 86:17
"Show me a sign for good, that those who hate me may see it and be ashamed, because You, Lord, have helped me and comforted me."

Being a walking, talking example of Christ's likeness is sometimes hard to do. To daily empty "self" of "self" and make room for the Holy Spirit to work within us is the key. I know you've heard that old saying stating what you put into something is exactly what you'll get out of it. As an addict, I never really comprehended how much this expression reflected life until now. In all my old behaviors, I put myself in precarious situations daily. I surrounded myself with bad people and bad habits like taking drugs, stealing, unprotected sex, swearing, and smoking. When everything around you is negative, it reflects in you as a person. This causes negative behaviors which show in all areas of your life; such as, your actions, speech, attitude, health, and appearance. Once I sobered up and started changing my companions, places and things, I noticed I was becoming a different person.

When we finally come around and desire to change our lives, we have what is called an "awakening." The Bible talks about this in Ephesians 5:8-14. *"For you were once darkness, but now you are light in the Lord. Walk as children of Light (for the fruit of the Spirit is in all goodness, righteousness, and truth), finding out what is acceptable to the Lord. And have no fellowship with the unfruitful works of darkness, but rather expose them. For it is shameful even to speak of those things which are done by them in secret. But all things that are exposed are made manifest by the light, for whatever makes manifest is light. Therefore, He says: 'Awake you who sleep, Arise from the dead, and Christ will give you light.'"*

These verses tell us exactly what God expects and bans us, as Christians, from indulging in: modern preoccupation with life and its struggles, perverted practices, and immoral behaviors

If we keep God as our focal point moment-to-moment, day-to-day, we will begin to reflect God in all we do. In turn, He will supply us with what we need to live a good and fruitful life. What does your life reflect, God or the world?

We are God's temple once we turn to Him. He wants us to keep our house (body and mind) clean.

I Corinthians 3:16-17
"Do you not know that you are the temple of God and that the Spirit of God dwells in you? If anyone defiles the temple of God, God will destroy him. For the temple of God is holy, which temple you are."

Please, my friends, think seriously about where you are and what you do today. When you start letting go of your old habits and old way of thinking, you make room for the "new man" to grow spiritually. This should not be an option but a necessity in all of our lives.

Prayer:

>Heavenly Father, I pray please help me to keep an open mind and heart to be able to learn from Christ's example that He has set for me to live by. Please open my eyes and ears to all You would have me learn from You daily. Show me as an example for good, oh Lord, help me to walk in Your footsteps. Amen

Day 10

"THE CHEATER"

Titus 3:2
"To speak evil of no one, to be peaceable, gentle, showing all humility to all men."

Are you dishonest? Are you a cheater, liar, or thief? This not only hurts you but others as well. From the time I started using drugs until I was sent to prison, I fell into all of these categories on a daily basis. My guilty conscience because of my lifestyle caused me to separate myself from God and my family. I felt I had cheated them all out of time, love, money, effort, and service.

When I was arrested, I began to seek answers on how to better myself. I no longer wanted to continue living the way I had been. Once I was transported to prison, I was put in a receiving lock-down unit. During this time, I came across a passage in the Bible that cut to the bone. I felt as if it was speaking to me on a personal level.

Romans 12:1-2
"I beseech you therefore, brethren, by the mercies of God, that you present your bodies a living sacrifice, holy, acceptable to God, which is your reasonable service. And do not be conformed to this world, but be transformed by the renewing of your mind, that you may prove what is that good and acceptable and perfect will of God."

No wonder I was a mess. I had not been doing this in my life at all.

After coming to a place of repentance through studying my Bible and church attendance, I had so many questions as we all do. Having presented myself to Christ and asking Him to become my Savior, I wondered, "Where do I go from here? What does God expect of me now?"

The Word, being the way to the truth, answers this plainly in Romans 12:9-18:

"Let love be without hypocrisy. Abhor (hate) what is evil. Cling to what is good. Be kindly affectionate to one another with brotherly love, in honor giving preference to one another; not lagging in diligence, fervent in spirit, serving the Lord; rejoicing in hope, patient in tribulation, continuing steadfastly in prayer; distributing to the needs of the saints, given to hospitality. Bless those who persecute you; bless and do not curse. Rejoice with those who rejoice, and weep with those who weep. Be of the same mind toward one another. Do not set your mind on high things, but associate with the humble. Do not be wise in your own opinion. Repay no one evil for evil. Have regard for good things in the sight of all men. If it is possible, as much as depends on you, live peaceably with all men."

This segment of the Bible clearly answers both questions of His expectations. I realized, at this point, I hadn't cheated God or my family - only myself.

REDEMPTION REMEMBERED

I give You my burdens, my sorrows and my strife,
In exchange You give me peace and love and eternal life.
As I rest in You, oh Lord, my joy and faith they grow,
In Your presence I have found salvation for my soul.
Your mercy and Your righteousness always shining true,

These are the things that I know will see me through.
I know the footprints in the sand are when You carried me,
Thanks to Your healing hand I'm no longer blind, I see.
My protector and my healer, my teacher and my friend,
To You I offer up my life – until the very end.

Prayer:
> Lord Jesus, I just want to ask You now to help me to hate what is evil, to cling to what is good, to be fervent in spirit, and steadfast in prayer. Let all my actions be a pleasure in Your sight. Amen

Day 11

"FORGIVENESS"

Psalm 103:12
"As far as the east is from the west, so far has He removed our transgressions from us."

God's forgiveness is probably the most incredible force in the universe. It stretches so far. It's made clear in God's Word that in order to receive all good things from Him, we must be living within His standards. God is always willing to forgive us, but we must live by His Word to the best of our ability. We must try to follow what He tells us to do. Matthew 6:14-15 says, *"For if you forgive men their trespasses, your heavenly Father will also forgive you. But if you do not forgive men their trespasses, neither will your heavenly Father forgive your trespasses."*

I know from experience that if you carry unforgiveness in your heart toward others, eventually, it will cause you to fall away from God, leading to sin. Unforgiveness comes in many forms. We must be aware of all types of unforgiveness. Some examples of this are holding grudges and judging others. Remember when we stand in unforgiveness, this can hinder our prayer life drastically, wreak havoc on personal relationships, and affect our family life. Love implies that we must respect others no matter what they do to us.

Matthew 5:44
"But I say to you, love your enemies, bless those who curse you, do good to those who hate you, and pray for those who spitefully use you and persecute you."

The Bible also tells us that we must learn not to judge each other or take out our anger on others but to forgive each other seventy times seven. I know we all often lose sight of God's will for us to love and forgive. When this happens, we, as human beings, get caught up in our own will, leading to weaknesses that bring about jealousy, envy, greed, and unforgiveness toward ourselves and others. We must learn to love and forgive despite how badly others may treat us or people we care about. We must learn to pardon in order to be pardoned from our own mistakes.

It says in Matthew 7:12, *"Therefore, whatever you want men to do to you, do also to them…"* When we were children, many of us learned this concept as the Golden Rule: "Do unto others whatever you would have them do unto you." It is that simple.

We must love our fellow man without judgment. In doing this in our lives, God will pardon us from our own iniquities when we pray sincerely and ask Him to. Now don't you think if He is willing to go to these lengths for us that the only sensible thing for us to do is show our fellow man that same respect?

Forgiveness reunites us to God through the blood of His Son, making it possible for us to be acceptable in His sight. Forgiveness is a gift, just like salvation, given to us at a great cost, Jesus' life. Think back to that day on the cross when Jesus said, *"Father, forgive them, for they do not know what they do"* (Luke 23:34). Should we not follow His example?

FORGIVEN

      F   For eternity you can dwell with Me if you repent from sin,

      O   Only believing in My sacrifice that I died and rose again.
      R   Realize that I am the resurrection and the light,
      G   God, He is your Father, in you He takes delight.
      I   I am always present, ever with you by your side,
      V   Victory is promised if in Me you will abide.
      E   Every time you stumble, keep your eyes on Me,
      N   Never doubt My love for you; please tell Me that you see.

My child, you're forgiven, My love for you is true,
No matter how many times you fall, I will see you through.

Prayer:
Lord, we come humbly to You and ask for a daily reprieve of our faults and mistakes. Please give us compassion and understanding so that we can learn to forgive and love others the way You forgive and love us. Lord, help our lives to be good examples of Your love and forgiveness for others and that those who hate and misunderstand us may see we have changed and repented of our old ways. Amen

Day 12

"HOPE"

Romans 8:24-25
"For we were saved in this hope, but hope that is seen is not hope; for why does one still hope for what he sees? But if we hope for what we do not see, we eagerly wait for it with perseverance."

God is telling us to have confidence in Him and His Word. The Lord wants us not to doubt Him or His abilities to control our lives in all situations, but to wait patiently keeping our eyes on Him.

Psalm 130:5
"I wait for the Lord, my soul waits, And in His word I do hope."

Hope is the trust that God will fulfill His promises to us in a way that leads us to true freedom in this lifetime and the next.

Psalm 130:7
"…hope in the Lord; for with the Lord there is mercy, and with Him is abundant redemption."

The person of wisdom lives in the moment with the knowledge and trust that all of life is in God's hands. Never give up your faith or your hope. With God as an active participant in your life, you are always in a "win-win" situation. God is looking out for the welfare of creation, and all people are guaranteed a bright future with hope if they stand strong in Christ.

Jeremiah 29:11

"For I know the thoughts that I think toward you, says the Lord, thoughts of peace and not of evil, to give you a future and a hope."

God gave Christ power over all things in this world and in the next, so when we put our hope in Him, we are guaranteed to be victorious.

HOPE

In my lifetime, I've put on so very many faces,
Looking for love and acceptance in all of the wrong places.
I tried every road, I searched high and I searched low,
Until I finally ran out of places I could go.
I was lost in darkness for years and for years,
Wallowing in my sorrow, my pity, and in fear.
It seemed the tears from my eyes always fell like constant rain,
I lived in misery and wallowed in pain.
Then one very special day I woke from my sleep,
I heard someone speak of Jesus and I felt my heart leap.
They said that there was joy and hope, could that possibly be?
Why would this man, Jesus, give His life for me?
I heard tell of forgiveness, of mercy and of love,
Some even spoke of eternity in Heaven up above.
So then I asked what the cost for all of this would be,
My friend said, "Are you kidding? It's all done for free!
A gift like this cannot be bought or even earned,
This is a lesson, my child, that you'll need to learn."
She told me, "Jesus died for me and that He rose again,
Giving us all victory until the very end."
I was told of the Spirit, the Father, and the Son,
And that if I would just believe we could be as one.
With this news, so overwhelmed, I fell to my knees,

Crying out and begging, "Tell me more – please, oh, please!"
She told me it was time to pray to the Father up above,
Asking for His forgiveness, His mercy, and His love.
She said, "It's so easy, please tell me that you see,
There's a plan and a purpose for you and for me.
If you'll just accept the price Jesus paid upon the cross,
You'll no longer live in darkness, feel scared or feel lost."
So my advice to all of you, every woman, every man,
Is give your heart to Jesus while you still can.

Prayer:
Father, we thank You that Your ways are higher than our ways. We thank You that we may have an understanding of Your plan for our future. Lord, we pray that our hope always rests in You. Amen

Day 13

"FAITH"

Jeremiah 32:27
"Behold, I am the Lord, the God of all flesh. Is there anything too hard for me?"

Stepping out in faith can be a very difficult task. I used to have a very hard time with faith. Believing in things unseen was not a reality for me. I guess you could say I was a "doubting Thomas." In John 20:24-29 and 31, Thomas doubts Christ's resurrection saying, *"'Unless I see in His hands the print of the nails, and put my finger into the print of the nails, and put my hand into His side, I will not believe.' And after eight days His disciples were again inside, and Thomas with them. Jesus came, the doors being shut, and stood in the midst, and said, 'Peace to you!' Then He said to Thomas, 'Reach your finger here, and look at my hands; and reach your hand here, and put it into My side. Do not be unbelieving, but believing.' And Thomas answered and said to Him, 'My Lord, and my God!' Jesus said to him, 'Thomas, because you have seen Me, you have believed. Blessed are those who have not seen and yet have believed'. . . believe that Jesus is the Christ, the Son of God, and that believing you may have life in His name."*

Jesus did so many miracles to instil faith in the people's hearts in the span of His lifetime that I can't even begin to cover them all. I truly advise you to read the New Testament. It will increase your faith and touch your heart.

Romans 10:17
"So then faith comes by hearing, and hearing by the word of God."

Isn't it time to watch your faith grow? I beg you, friends, to step out in faith.

Grow in your knowledge of God's Word. Trust in our Savior, Christ Jesus – He loves you!

"I HAVE ALWAYS BEEN," SAYS THE LORD

I have always been with you, and I will always be,
I will give you strength and life; just keep your eyes on me.
I will be your counselor, and I will be your friend,
I will guide you and I will keep you from now until the end.
I will be your healer and comfort you in pain,
I will walk with you every hour through the darkness and rain.
When all the storms and trials of life seem too much to bear,
You'll never have to look too far for I'm already there.
I have always been with you and I will always be,
The price is paid; the battle is won, just put your faith in Me.

Prayer:
Lord, in You and only You, I put my trust. Give me faith in Jesus' name. I praise You for all the battles You have won for me, for in You I am strong. In Your name, Jesus, I will walk in faith and claim victory over fear, anger, addiction, sickness, and all other worldly things. Amen

Day 14

"HEALING AND RESTORATION"

Psalm 103:2-4
"Bless the Lord, O my soul, and forget not all His benefits: Who forgives all your iniquities, Who heals all your diseases, Who redeems your life from destruction, Who crowns you with loving kindness and tender mercies."

When I was arrested, I was very sick from HIV and Hepatitis C. Over time, God has stabilized these issues. When we stay safely within the confinement of God's love, He promises protection, healing, and restoration.

Today I can thank Him, not only for saving my soul, but for restoring my health as well. Thank You, Jesus, that by Your stripes we are healed. The presence of God in your life can restore your soul, strengthen your mind, and revitalize your health as it has mine.

Psalm 91:9-11
"Because you have made the Lord, who is my refuge, Even the Most High, your dwelling place, no evil shall befall you, nor shall any plague come near your dwelling; For He shall give His angels charge over you, To keep you in all your ways."

This passage is a precious promise from God. But take notice that it also has stipulations. It tells us from the very beginning that we must put God first in our lives. He plainly says this promise is conditional on me making the Lord my refuge and my habitation. We must learn to do this and live by His Word. If we do, He promises to heal us of all things – addictions included! Praise God through Him there is deliverance!

Psalm 107:19-20

"Then they cried out to the Lord in their trouble, and He saved them out of their distresses. He sent His word and healed them, and delivered them from their destructions."

Isaiah 61:1 states, *"The Spirit of the Lord God is upon Me, Because the Lord has anointed Me to preach good tidings to the poor; He has sent Me to heal the brokenhearted, to proclaim liberty to the captives, And the opening of the prison to those who are bound."* In the New Testament, Jesus read these words to the people who were in the temple and then said, *"Today this scripture is fulfilled in your hearing"* (Luke 4:21). Jesus was saying that in Him all these promises were being fulfilled. These promises of healing, liberty, and freedom are available to you through Him! Seek Jesus with all of your heart and trust God's Word and He will heal you physically, mentally, and emotionally. This includes addiction, a broken heart, illness, unforgiveness, guilt and anything else you can think of.

God is an all knowing, all loving, all seeing, and all forgiving God. If you just listen carefully, the Holy Spirit will guide and instruct you in the path that leads to healing, righteousness, strength, joy, and more.

GRATITUDE

Thank You, Lord, for your daily bread and all the wisdom that is told,
Thank You for your forgiveness and mercy and promises you uphold.
As I read Your Word and learn more everyday about Your love so true,
Thank You, Jesus, for dying for me; I want to live for You.

The Father, the Son, and the Holy Spirit all being one and the same,
Only this Trinity can save my life – not money, not fortune, nor fame.
All of these things I strove to get and tried so hard to possess,
None of them brought me any real joy or happiness.
So when all is said and worldly things have disappeared and gone away,
I'll stand before my Lord and God and to Him I'll say,
"Please save the souls, dear Jesus, of all the ones I love,
And take to heart my enemies and pardon them with love.
I pray for all the lost ones, Lord, I know you love them too,
I only hope they still have time to pray and turn to you."

Prayer:
Dear Jesus, thank You for binding up our hearts, our bodies, and our minds and healing us with Your love. Thank You for restoring me, Lord. Help me show my gratitude by serving you more faithfully each day in my daily life through fervent prayer and meditation on Your Word. Help me to share my time and resources with others, especially those in need. Amen

Day 15

"FELLOWSHIP"

II Corinthians 6:14
"Do not be unequally yoked together with unbelievers. For what fellowship has righteousness with lawlessness? And what communion has light with darkness?"

I believe we are all looking to be loved and accepted. But we must be careful where we seek to fulfill these needs. Fellowship is human nature – wanting to connect with another person, wanting someone to talk to, someone who can relate to us for who we are is natural. If you look at your life closely, you will notice that the people you surround yourself with affect how you live. God wants us to have fellowship in our lives with people we are equally "yoked" with.

When you surround yourself with other Christians, you will find that you can exhort one another, encouraging each other to walk upright and by God's Word. If you fall, your Christian friends will help you up and give you the support you need until you can walk on your own again. But if you constantly surround yourself with ungodly people who are living in sin, very soon you will be living an ungodly lifestyle too. People are like chameleons. They tend to change to fit into whatever environment they are in. If addicts choose to live in a drug house, they will begin to use again. When removed from that situation to an opposite environment with people who are walking a positive road, the whole scenario changes.

Ephesians 5:15
"See then that you walk circumspectly, not as fools but as wise, redeeming the time, because the days are evil."

This is telling us we should be mindful of the company we keep. We should watch our path to avoid contact with undesirable influences. God wants us to fellowship with others who will uplift our spirit and direct us on a path toward Him.

I John 1:6-7
"If we say that we have fellowship with Him, and walk in darkness, we lie and do not practice the truth. But if we walk in the light as He is in the light, we have fellowship with one another, and the blood of Jesus Christ His Son cleanses us from all sin."

Surround yourself with love and light, my friends. Choose your relationships wisely. Remember you are responsible for the company you keep.

Prayer:
>Heavenly Father, give me a spirit of discernment to know when I am in a positive, productive relationship so that through fellowship I may grow. Amen

Day 16

"CHOICES"

Acts 2:21
"And it shall come to pass that whoever calls on the name of the Lord shall be saved."

Some days you may feel defeated or alone, like you have no one to turn to. Nothing could be further from the truth. God is bigger than any problem you have. Whoever or whatever is opposing you cannot stand against God. Everything we face in life is about choice: right or wrong, joy or pain, happiness or sadness, faith or doubt, love or hate, truth or lie, God or Satan, life or death… God gives us free will to choose what we want for our lives - good or bad.

Trying to make sure all your choices are based on pure motives can be very difficult. When you have a difficult decision to make in any circumstance, always pray about it and ask God to help you make the right choice. Follow the prompting of your heart rather than the desires of your flesh.

If you make a mistake by choosing poorly, take responsibility for it and ask for forgiveness. Our God is a God of many chances. Through God's Word, we have the knowledge and wisdom to make appropriate decisions in all situations that affect our lives. We must learn to train ourselves to refer to the Word of God in every situation we face.

Psalm 37:23-24
The steps of a good man are ordered by the Lord, And He delights in his way. Though he fall, he shall not be utterly cast down; For the Lord upholds him with His hand."

Psalm 18:30
"As for God, His way is perfect; The word of the Lord is proven; He is a shield to all who trust in Him."

Each day when I remind myself to place my trust in God, in His promises, and in His love, I find it easier to make positive choices in my life.

ME AMOUR, MY LORD

> I worship and adore you, Lord; I praise your mighty name.
> I put no one else before you, Lord, your promises I claim.
> Promises of healing, of forgiveness and of love,
> Promises of protection from heaven up above.
> Your Word I've hidden in my heart to give me hope and keep me strong,
> To help me keep my eyes on You and teach me right from wrong.
> An indwelling of Your spirit for this I truly pray,
> To keep me and to guide me every single day.
> I give myself in complete surrender, a sacrifice to Thee,
> For all the mercy, grace, and love that You've shown to me.
> On my knees before You, I open up my soul,
> Knowing only You, Lord, can truly make me whole.
> I dedicate myself to You, a vessel for You to fill,
> I only live to please You, Lord, and mind Your perfect will.
> So that when my life is over and I stand before Your Son.
> He'll wrap His loving arms around me and tell me, "Job well done!"

Prayer:

Dear Jesus, I ask that You teach me and help me submit to the Holy Spirit's nudging and whisperings. Help me to discern Your voice in my heart when I make choices in my life. Let me be sensitive to Your needs and Your desires for me today and everyday. Thank You for Your mercy and understanding of my faults. Help me to always look toward You. Amen

Day 17

"JOY"

John 16:24
"Until now you have asked nothing in My name. Ask, and you will receive, that your joy may be full."

When I was running "full throttle" in my addiction, I had no real joy. Any "happy" moments I had were very temporary, shallow, and short lived. I was constantly worried about tomorrow and what it would present. Does this sound familiar to you?

Matthew 6:25-26
"Therefore I say to you, do not worry about your life, what you will eat or what you will drink; nor about your body, what you will put on. Is not life more than food and the body more than clothing? Look at the birds of the air, for they neither sow nor reap nor gather into barns; yet your heavenly Father feeds them. Are you not of more value than they?"

Even though God instructs us not to worry about tomorrow, this can be very hard to do. Learning to place our problems and our burdens in God's hands is much easier said than done. When people tell us not to worry and that things will get better, we tend to dwell on those things even more. Little did I realize that all the worrying I was doing was robbing me of my joy.

Worry also wreaks havoc on your spiritual life because you are failing to trust God. Philippians 4:6-7 states, *"Be anxious for nothing, but in everything by prayer and supplication, with thanksgiving, let your requests be made known to God; and the peace of God which surpasses all understanding, will guard your hearts and minds through Christ Jesus."* What a wonderful promise! Satan will try to steal your joy by throwing stumbling blocks in your path. Not to worry, though, because Jesus has given us victory over the devil through the sacrifice He made for us.

Nehemiah 8:10
"...Do not sorrow, for the joy of the Lord is your strength."

Psalm 16:11
"You will show me the path of life; In Your presence is fullness of joy; At Your right hand are pleasures forevermore."

I Peter 5:7
"Casting all your care upon Him, for He cares for you."

Psalm 55:22
"Cast your burden on the Lord, And He shall sustain you; He shall never permit the righteous to be moved."

Isaiah 26:3
"You will keep him in perfect peace, Whose mind is stayed on You, Because he trusts in You."

ULTIMATE SACRIFICE

When I think about the loss of Your life upon the cross:
The anguish You felt, the torture, the pain,
All you withstood was for my life's gain.

The blood You shed upon that tree,
To loose my bonds and set me free.
The holy sacrifice that You made,
The ultimate price that You gladly paid.
What You did on Calvary has such significance to me!

My eyes toward Heaven, I praise your name,
I thank you, Jesus, that You came.
I praise You, Father, for making me whole,
Everything You did to save my eternal soul.
Without You, Lord, I would be lost,
But You came to earth and paid the cost.
My life I dedicate to You,
Just tell me, Lord what to do.
I love you…

Prayer:
Jesus, help me to remember to cast all my cares upon You. Keep me from the sin of worry, Lord, and restore my joy. I pray for constant remembrance through Your spirit to always turn to You, not just in times of trouble but also in times of joy. Empower me through Your Holy Spirit, Lord. For, truly, the joy of the Lord is my strength. Thank You for Your compassion, concern, overflowing joy, and everlasting love.
Amen

Day 18

"A HUMBLING EXPERIENCE"

James 4:10
"Humble yourselves in the sight of the Lord, and He will lift you up."

Alcoholics Anonymous has many steps in their recovery program. Being humble and asking God to remove shortcomings is one part of it. This can be an issue for us as addicts because self-centeredness is a very real problem. We tend to think the whole world revolves around us and what we want. Relying on someone else for anything is unheard of. We get stuck in a "me, me, me" mode and "self" is all we think about.

Learning to step outside of ourselves and think of others first is a very important part of recovery from any addiction. This includes sharing our experience, strength, and hope with others. When we do this, it helps us to set aside some of our selfishness and pride and become more aware of our fellow man.

It is important to remember that we are all children of God, and He expects no less of us than He is willing to give Himself. We need to learn to love all mankind showing no partiality. Sometimes it can be difficult to humble ourselves; it seems easier to put ourselves on a pedestal looking down at everyone else around us. We tend to try and build ourselves up in others' eyes, when what we need to consider is that man's opinion of us has no bearing on eternity or where we will spend it. The Lord's opinion of us is what counts.

Philippians 2:4

"Let each of you look out not only for his own interests, but also for the interests of others."

Jesus will someday hold us accountable for all of our actions and attitudes. On that note, let us follow the advice we find in God's Word and humble ourselves before Him; and in turn, He will bless us.

THE PERFECT TRINITY

As I come into your presence, Lord, I give You all my praise,
I only wish to worship You the rest of all my days.
I come humbly before You, I give You my heart,
From Your sweet presence, Jesus, I never want to part.
Forgiveness from the Father, love from the Son,
Guidance from the Spirit until my life is done.
This is all I can hope for to be given to me,
Only these things will truly set me free.

Prayer:
Lord, we ask You to help us to be humble, thinking of others before ourselves. Let us always consider Your opinion as the most important one in our lives. Help us, Father, to live within the boundaries You set for us so that You can lift us up in due time. I thank You that through the strength You provide I am able to cope with problems I face every day of my brief life. I praise You for my new awareness of my need to help others instead of always helping myself. Amen

Day 19

"IMPORTANT RELATIONSHIPS"

Lamentations 3:24
"'The Lord is my portion,' says my soul, 'Therefore I hope in Him.'"

As an addict, I know that I have always had a difficult time distinguishing which relationships in my life are important. Most of the choices I made as priorities for my life were very poor choices. I used to think that boyfriends, friends, and then family were all I needed. I rated these relationships as the most important and in that order. This line of thinking is wrong.

As I sobered up and came out of the haze I was living in, my priorities began to change. I realized that most of the people I thought I needed had deserted me. Those who truly loved me, like my family, I had abandoned.

When I looked around for someone to turn to for help, Jesus was the only one left standing there with open arms. Moving further into my recovery, I began to acknowledge Christ as my "higher power." Waiting to embrace me with His love and forgiveness, Jesus was the only one who could uphold me in my worst times of weakness and despair.

To my fellow addicts in all walks of life, I must say, "Don't fret." There is hope for you no matter what you've done. You need only to ask in order to receive (Matthew 7:7-8). God will never reject you, ridicule you, or abandon you. Though we have all made poor choices by defiling our bodies, in more ways than one, God's love is so perfect that He still welcomes us to come to Him. God's desire is for us to have a personal relationship with Him. When we finally realize that we've "screwed up" our lives so badly that we're only hanging on by a thread, all we need to do is call on Jesus.

Jesus is our lifeline to God. He saves us before that thread breaks and we fall. Through His blood shed on the cross, we are forgiven, saved, healed, loved, renewed, and strengthened. My point is that the only relationship we need to rate as number one in our lives is our relationship with Christ. Survival through our addiction and our recovery depends upon Him; He is our portion.

FRIEND OR FOE

> Grace and mercy I receive through Your sacrifice,
> salvation I receive through Your love,
> Protection and healing are other gifts given from Heaven above,
> Through the power of Your resurrection, every path's been paved,
> You must choose the road you wish to follow, a decision must be made.
> The choice won't be easy, there's temptation around every bend,
> It makes it hard to determine who is a foe or who is a friend.
> But I have something to share with you that you can share with another,

Jesus, my friend, will see you through and stick closer to you than a brother.
He'll never abandon you; He'll uphold every promise and listen whenever you cry,
He'll hold your hand and ease every fear; He'll answer every question of "Why?"
A perfect mate, husband, lover, protector, healer, and friend,
Jesus is the answer; He's true to the very end.
So when you make a decision on which road you will go,
Think very carefully who you will choose, will it be friend or foe?

Prayer:
Lord Jesus, thank You for Your loyalty to me as my Savior, my brother, my confidant, and my friend. Thank You for Your acceptance, Your love, Your forgiveness and Your grace. I pray through the empowerment of the Holy Spirit I can learn to put You first in my life above all others. Amen

Matthew 7:7-8
"Ask, and it will be given to you; seek, and you will find; knock, and it will be opened to you. For everyone who asks receives, and he who seeks finds, and to him who knocks it will be opened."

Day 20

"SOWING AND REAPING"

Galatians 6:7-8
"Do not be deceived, God is not mocked; for whatever a man sows, that he will also reap. For he who sows to his flesh will of the flesh reap corruption, but he who sows to the Spirit will of the Spirit reap everlasting life."

I'm sure you've heard the expression "what you sow is what you reap." No matter what you do in life, the amount of effort you put into any situation will be reflected in the end result or circumstance. Any choices you make, good or bad, will have corresponding consequences.

When I was using drugs, any negative situation I ended up in started with a negative action on my part. I reaped what I sowed. In recovery, the same theory applies. The seeds you sow in your recovery will determine the success of your sobriety. The three major seeds of growth you need are honesty, acceptance, and love.

Be honest with yourself and others at all times; accept that you cannot be successful without including God in your life; and love yourself and others with a Christ-like love.
These are all positive seeds that when planted will reap positive fruits in your life.
Learning to love, being honest, and admitting you need help may not be easy, but these are all steps in the right direction. Walking through these steps on a daily basis will get easier as you practice them. Pray and ask God to help you; He will.

Philippians 1:6

"...being confident of this very thing, that He who has begun a good work in you will complete it until the day of Christ Jesus."

Remember, you reap what you sow and <u>any</u> seed planted will bear fruit...good or bad. With God's strength and direction in your life, you can choose to plant positive seeds which will bear positive fruit.

THE FATHER'S GARDEN

> Inside my heart there's a beautiful place I never thought could be,
> Like a garden in the spring time, there's new growth that I can see.
> Honesty, love, and acceptance causes me to grow,
> Producing faith, love, and hope I never thought I would know.
> As the seasons continue passing, the fruits of the Spirit bloom,
> What started in a single seed is now a garden neatly groomed.
> Pruned by the Father, nurtured by the Son,
> Fruits of the Spirit produce unity so we can be as one.

Prayer:
Lord Jesus help me to lay aside all that is evil and sinful in Your sight. Teach me about honesty, love, and acceptance. Help me to plant only good things in my life and in the lives of others. I want to reap what I sow, Lord. Help me to remain in Christ at all times, living appropriately under Your instruction, reaping all the blessings You bestow upon Your children. I ask this in Jesus' name. Amen

Galatians 5:22-23
"But the fruit of the Spirit is love, joy, peace, long suffering, kindness, goodness, faithfulness, gentleness, self-control. Against such there is no law."

Colossians 1:10-11
"...that you may walk worthy of the Lord, fully pleasing Him, being fruitful in every good work and increasing in the knowledge of God; strengthened with all might, according to His glorious power..."

II Samuel 22:33
> *"God is my strength and power, And He makes my way perfect."*

Day 21

"SALVATION, THE FREE GIFT"

Psalm 91:16
"With long life I will satisfy him, and show him My salvation."

Salvation through Jesus is God's gift to us as His children. Never in life will anyone offer you anything that is worth more than the gift of salvation. Salvation cannot be bought or even earned but is given free of charge – all we have to do is accept it. Our salvation was bought and paid for with Jesus' life.

John 3:16-17
"For God so loved the world that He gave His only begotten Son, that whoever believes in Him should not perish but have everlasting life. For God did not send His Son into the world to condemn the world, but that the world through Him might be saved."

When we were actively living in addiction, the Bible described us in Titus 3:3 as, *"…foolish, disobedient, deceived, serving various lusts and pleasures, living in malice and envy, hateful and hating one another."* We must be willing to deny our "old nature" by giving up old habits and behaviors

Titus 2:11-14
"For the grace of God that brings salvation has appeared to all men, teaching us that, denying ungodliness and worldly lusts, we should live soberly, righteously, and godly in the present age, looking for the blessed hope and glorious appearing of our great God and Savior Jesus Christ, who gave Himself for us, that He might redeem us from every lawless deed and purify for Himself His own special people,…"

Do you see your need for Jesus? Do you believe Him and His Word? John 11:25-26 says, *"Jesus said to her, 'I am the resurrection and the life. He who believes in Me, though he may die, he shall live. And whoever lives and believes in Me shall never die. Do you believe this?'"*

Romans 10:9-10
"...that if you confess with your mouth the Lord Jesus and believe in your heart that God has raised Him from the dead, you will be saved. For with the heart one believes unto righteousness, and with the mouth confession is made unto salvation."

In an earlier daily reading, "Commitment and Prayer" (Day 4), I wrote a prayer that you could pray to receive salvation. If you did not pray that prayer when you read that lesson but want to pray now, just simply talk to Jesus and say, "I recognize I need You in my life. I am ready to trust You. I believe You are the Son of God who lived, died, and rose again, and I accept You as my Savior. Please help me. I want to live a life that pleases You. Amen"

If you prayed the prayer of salvation, you now belong to God. You are His child! And because you have accepted Christ as the Son of God and asked Him into your life, you immediately become eligible for all of God's promises written in His Word. Read the Bible* and find out what this means to you. Jesus will help you to live according to His Word. He will create in you a "new heart" and a "new nature" leaving behind the old one and its destructive behaviors

Learning to trust Christ with our lives, families, jobs, and finances is a part of our salvation. Nothing we try to accomplish on our own will give us success over our addictions or the strength to live our lives for God. Only with the direction of God's Word, our relationship with Jesus through prayer, and the leading of the Holy Spirit in our lives, will we mature in our "walk" to make the right decisions that bring us joy and peace in this life and an eternity of happiness in the next. Remember always that through our faith in Christ, we have victory over anything we may face – He is our deliverer!

Psalm 37:39-40
"But the salvation of the righteous is from the Lord; He is their strength in the time of trouble. And the Lord shall help them and deliver them; He shall deliver them from the wicked, And save them, Because they trust in Him."

Titus 3:4-7
"But when the kindness and the love of God our Savior toward man appeared, not by works of righteousness which we have done, but according to His mercy He saved us, through the washing of regeneration and renewing of the Holy Spirit, whom He poured out on us abundantly through Jesus Christ our Savior, that having been justified by His grace we should become heirs according to the hope of eternal life."

FATHER GOD

Father God, before you on my knees I pray
For your guidance and protection to keep me through the day.
Father God, I'm asking for renewed mercies from above.

Father God, forgive my sins and shower me in love.
Father God, I thank you for never leaving me.
Father God, I thank you for Your son on Calvary.
I'm putting all my faith in You for You are the great "I AM",
The Holy One, the Lion of Judah, the sacrificial Lamb.
Your death and resurrection for all the world to see
Would inspire such a growth of faith throughout eternity.
Father God, we praise You for helping us to see
That all we need is faith in You for You to set us free!

Prayer:
Thank You, Lord, for the sacrifice You made for us that through Your death and resurrection, we are a saved people. Knowing this, Lord, I come before you just as I am. I need Your love and forgiveness, guidance, and wisdom. Please, Lord, guide me on the path I must walk today. In Jesus' name I ask this. Amen

*As a new Christian, when you start reading the Bible, choose a version that is easy to understand. I read and study the New King James Version (NKJV) of the Bible. I have used this version for the scripture references in this book. The New King James Version (NKJV), the New American Standard (NAS), and the New International Version (NIV) are all trusted versions of the Bible that are translated from the original King James Version (KJV) but are written in modern day English. Many churches and organizations (such as <u>The Gideons</u>) will give you a free Bible to read if you do not have one.

I recommend that you start reading in the New Testament. This tells of the life of Jesus; what He accomplished for us through His life, death, and resurrection; and shows us how to live as a Christian. The Gospel of John is a great "book" to start reading because it emphasizes the great, unfailing love Jesus has for us.

Day 22

"From Desire to Destiny"

Psalm 145:16-20
"You open Your hand and satisfy the desire of every living thing. The Lord is righteous in all His ways, Gracious in all His works. The Lord is near to all who call upon Him, To all who call upon Him in truth. He will fulfill the desire of those who fear (respect, to stand in awe of, love) Him; He also will hear their cry and save them. The Lord preserves all who love Him, But all the wicked He will destroy."

To fulfill your destiny is to realize your heart's innermost desires and dreams. Ask yourself, "What do I truly desire in life? What can I do to achieve my dreams?" My answer to you is to put your faith in God's perfect plan for your destiny.

There will be times in your life when you are facing a crisis or a problem that is too big for you to handle. During these times, you must trust and have faith in the fact that Jesus has a plan for each of our lives. Look beyond the circumstances you may be facing to the desired outcome of the situation you are in. Through faith, strive to reach that outcome at all costs.

We all need to live each day as though it were our last, looking toward Jesus to fulfill our desires and dreams. We've all heard the analogy "ask and you shall receive" (Matthew 7:7). Throughout the Bible, God lets us know that He wants us to come to Him with our needs, desires, hopes, and dreams. We need to call on Him for everything. We need to place all of our requests in His capable hands.

Your priorities and attitudes will determine the choices you make which directly affects the direction of your life. In Matthew 23:37-39, Jesus said, *"You shall love the Lord your God with all your heart, with all your soul, and with all your mind. This is the first and great commandment. And the second is like it: You shall love your neighbor as yourself."* It is important to extend your hand in love to those who cross your path every day for this is the Lord's command and, often, His greatest test. By giving God His rightful place in your life and by loving others, you will be obeying God. When you honor God and His priorities in your life, He will fulfill your destiny, and your dreams will become a reality.

Psalm 37:4-5
"Delight yourself also in the Lord, And He shall give you the desires of your heart. Commit your way to the Lord, Trust also in Him, And He shall bring it to pass."

YOUR DESIRE BEGETS YOUR DESTINY

Look to Me, My child. Don't you know that your desires, intense passions, and yearnings are the things I wish to fulfill? Please realize the dreams you dream, I put in your heart. My child, the anticipation of perfect love and acceptance come from Me. I only wish you to experience life in its fullest embodiment.

When in doubt of My perfect will for you, persevere in faith and know that in every life circumstance there is an opportunity for growth. This growth is needed to realize your dreams and make them a reality. In my perfect plan for you, the realization of your dreams fulfills all passions, yearnings and desires. Set your goals high and press through your challenging circumstances to victory.

ALWAYS REMEMBER

Always remember in any situation and under every circumstance,
I will be Your Protector and Provider.
Each day that passes and each night as you sleep,
I am always and forever by your side.
I have never left you and never will leave you,
Nothing you do or say will cause Me to love you any less.
Always remember, you are not alone or abandoned,
Because I am everywhere at all times.
All that is required is for you to call on My name,
I will always hear you.
Do you not know that I am your Creator and your Father?
I was there when you were born.
Do you not understand that I created you to be just the way you are when you trust and abide in Me?
Always remember, I love you unconditionally.
Seek and you shall find Me,
Knock and it shall be opened for you,
Ask and you will receive.

Why?
Because I am your Father…and because I love you!

Jeremiah 1:5
"Before I formed you in the womb I knew you; Before you were born I sanctified you;
I ordained you a prophet to the nations."

Isaiah 43:1
"But now, thus says the Lord, who created you...And He who formed you...'Fear not, for I have redeemed you; I have called you by your name; You are Mine.'"

Prayer
> Lord, help me to daily focus on You and Your will for me despite any circumstances I may face. Help me to realize that growth is part of life. Give me the strength to believe and strive for my dreams and the hope for a better tomorrow--no matter what I may face today. Let my actions reflect Your love in all I do. Amen

Day 23

"ADVERSITIES"

Life is often filled with adversity and problems which can deepen our faith; they do not have to destroy us! Through testing and trials, Christ can be made real and magnified in our lives. Remember as you read this and think about your own life, that Jesus also suffered adversity, self-discipline, trials, and temptations. Through your own adversity, God can help you perceive life from His perspective, and thus enjoy more of His presence and power.

Problems and adversities in our lives are often very hard for us to understand. We want our lives to go along smoothly "without a hitch." We must remember that everyone, Christian or not, struggles with life's problems and adversities. Through our struggle with adversity, sometimes we win and sometimes we fail. Our only recourse is to trust God and believe His Word is true!

Reading God's Word, especially the Psalms, is a real comfort during problems and adversity. Psalm 31 is called "The Lord a Fortress in Adversity." Psalm 31:7-8 states, *"I will be glad and rejoice in Your mercy, For You have considered my trouble; You have known my soul in adversities, and have not shut me up into the hand of the enemy; You have set my feet in a wide place."*

We all have issues in our lives that we face such as illness, depression, addictions, family issues, marital problems, and financial disasters. Adversities are all the problems, trials, and tribulations we go through in life that shape us into who we are. It comes in many forms, big and small, and we face it on a daily basis. Many of the things we face are in fact lessons we should use to teach us to rely on Christ in our times of weakness.

In II Corinthians 12:9 the Lord tells Paul (a follower of Jesus), *"My grace is sufficient for you, for My strength is made perfect in weakness."* Paul pleaded with God to take the adversity he was facing away and God said, "No." God wanted Paul to lean on Him so that the power of Christ might rest on him.

The purpose of adversity is to help shape us daily to be more subservient, obedient, humble, compassionate, empathetic, and loving. Each time we overcome a trial and learn the lesson within it, we become more like Christ. It is God's way of molding us slowly into His image.

Although suffering is hard, if perceived from God's perspective, it can result in the ability to persevere (to continue in spite of all things.) Through perseverance, a believer's faith can grow and he or she becomes more stable and more deeply rooted in Jesus.

We all have the strength to resist and overcome anything when we submit ourselves fully to God. The Bible confirms this in James 4:7-8, *"Therefore submit to God. Resist the devil and he will flee from you. Draw near to God and He will draw near to you..."* It also states that when we are weak, He is strong (I Corinthians 4:10). By submission to Christ, when we overcome whatever trial we are facing, God can be magnified through our lives.

We need to be steadfast in purpose, focusing our faith and trust during any troubles we face—knowing that we have victory through Christ! When we do this, we become winners, "over-comers", and a living demonstration of God's supernatural power in action. You must remember no matter what you are facing today: The Lord cares about everything you face because you are precious in His sight.

Romans 8:28 states, *"And we know that all things work together for good to those who love God, to those who are called according to His purpose."* Memorize this verse and it will give you great strength to endure whatever life throws at you.

HIS PRECIOUS TREASURE

The rich, the poor, the young and the old, He knows them all by name,
The sick and the well, the good and the bad, for each one He came.
Every life and every soul is precious in God's sight,
He gave His only begotten Son so we might live life right.
Each time we stumble or get lost in sin, a light for our path He will be,
He will tend each one's needs; He will heal our hurts and open blind eyes to see.
Each life is a gem in the Father's sight, precious as a diamond even though rough,
Cherished and treasured until life's end when we've finally been polished enough.
Through trials we're sculpted and perfectly cut until before the Father we stand,
A jewel and a treasure where we finally belong, home in the Promised Land.

Prayer

Lord, in You I put my trust today. I praise You for all the battles You have won for me. Thank You that I am strong because of who You are and for what You have done for me. I ask in child-like faith to be able to endure life's trials, temptations, and storms. Thank you, Lord, for Your strength in my times of weakness. Amen

Day 24

"SIN IN OUR LIVES"

Romans 6:23
"For the wages of sin is death, but the gift of God is eternal life in Christ Jesus our Lord."

Sin is any thought, word, action, omission, or desire contrary to the law of God. All sin is evil in God's eyes and no one sin is greater than another. Sin is sin!

Scripture says transgression of the law is sin (I John 3:4); all unrighteousness is sin (I John 5:17); showing partiality is sin (James 2:8-9); knowing to do good and not doing it is sin (James 4:17) – the list is endless. Fortunately, we serve a merciful God who loves us despite our sinful nature.

Romans 3:23
"For all have sinned and fall short of the glory of God."

I John 1:9 says, *"If we confess our sins, He is faithful and just to forgive us our sins and to cleanse us from all unrighteousness."* Any sin committed must be confronted and confessed in order to be forgiven. Why? Because sin can hinder our relationship with God and close off our prayer life. This is a dangerous way to live. An unconfessed sin makes us feel guilty and often leads us to more unacceptable behaviors

We must be open and honest with our Savior in order for our consciences to be clear and our hearts to be pure. If our conscience is clear, we can come to the Lord with perfect assurance and trust that He will hear our petitions. He hears what we ask of Him because we are striving to obey His law and doing the things that please Him. There are many blessings that come because we confess our sins.

Psalm 32:1-5
"Blessed is he whose transgression is forgiven, whose sin is covered. Blessed is the man to whom the Lord does not impute iniquity (sin); and in whose spirit there is no deceit. When I kept silent, my bones grew old through my groaning all the day long. For day and night Your hand was heavy upon me; my vitality was turned into the drought of summer. I acknowledged my sin to You, and my iniquity I have not hidden. I said, 'I will confess my transgressions to the Lord,' and You forgave the iniquity of my sin."

Psalm 32:10
Many sorrows shall be to the wicked; But he who trusts in the Lord, mercy shall surround him."

Have you experienced the joy of a relationship with God through the forgiveness of your sins? If not, humble yourself, acknowledge your inability to pay the debt of your sin. Ask God to forgive you and accept His forgiveness. When you accept Christ's sacrifice, you begin to experience a freedom that I cannot explain.

GOD'S PROMISE

When I woke this morning the Lord whispered in my ear,
I had to lay there quietly to make sure I could hear.

He told me that He loved me despite of all I'd done,
And that my life was far from over, it had only just begun.
A plan and a purpose, not only just for me,
But for all of God's creations, if only they would see.
He said set your eyes upon me and blessing from above,
Call upon the Father and His perfect love.
I will heal you and keep you, and take your away your pain,
The tears from your eyes will no longer fall like rain.
My mercy and My forgiveness will finally make you whole,
Child, please accept my sacrifice for it will save your soul.
In your weakness, I will strengthen, and in darkness, I'll give light,
Can't you see, My child, you are precious in My sight.
My only Son I gave for you to die upon that tree,
Can't you see, My child, He came to set you free.
I'm begging you to take a stand just one time in your life,
Let Me shoulder all your burdens, your worries, and your strife.
Take My yoke upon you, your burdens will be light,
And realize when things go wrong, only I can make them right.
Patiently, I'll wait for you, ever by your side,
Until you call upon My name and no longer wish to hide.

> Put down your masks of anger, of resentment, and of fear,
> Reach out your hand, call My name, and know that I am here.
> I have never left you, if only you would see,
> I'm ever here beside you, if you'll just call and lean on Me.
> Can't you see, all My children, you are precious in My sight,
> And each and every one of you has a future so very bright.

Psalm 103:2-4
"Bless the Lord, O my soul, and forget not all His benefits: Who forgives all your iniquities, Who heals all your diseases, Who redeems your life from destruction, Who crowns you with loving kindness and tender mercies."

Prayer:
> Father, we thank You for loving us so much that You were willing to make the ultimate sacrifice. Thank You for salvation and eternal life through Jesus Christ Your Son. Thank You for Your amazing grace, unfathomable love and never ending forgiveness. I lift up holy hands and a grateful heart to praise Your name. Amen

Day 25

"THE WITNESS"

Isaiah 6:8
"I heard the voice of the Lord saying: 'Whom shall I send, and who will go for Us?' Then I said, 'Here I am! Send me.'"

I have found that being a walking testimony of God's grace in action has been a huge step in my recovery. In many recovery programs, they talk about sharing your experience, strength, and hope with others. As a Christian in recovery, we must do the same. No matter where we are or what our situation is we need to speak boldly of the Lord Jesus and of all He's done for us.

Even when I was in prison, I found that I had a tremendous opportunity to witness for Christ by sharing my experiences with other women. No part played in spreading the news of God's love and salvation is too small. Being a good example for others is also part of being a witness for Christ.

In Ephesians 4:29 it says, *"Let no corrupt word proceed out of your mouth, but what is good for necessary edification, that it may impart grace to the hearers."* By sharing your testimony with someone else, you may actually save their life. Jesus can use you any where and at any time if you will let Him. As a Christian in recovery, we need to follow the example set by Jesus as closely as we can. If we want to live a Spirit-filled life, we need to follow Him one step at a time always basing our actions on the Bible and its God-breathed advice on how to behave as His beloved children. The best way to witness for Him is being a walking, talking example of God's grace every day.

Matthew 5:16
"Let your light so shine before men, that they may see your good works and glorify your Father in Heaven."

"WHO WILL GO?"

When my life finally quieted down, the Father took me by the hand.
As we walked, I heard Him ask, "Who will go and share the Promised Land?"
"The Promised Land?" I asked Him. What message could this be?
"Walk with Me a moment," He said, "then you'll plainly see."
A moment became a day, and a day became a year,
And being a faithful Father, He was always near.
I learned many lessons of laughter, love, and pain,
And when I'd fall, He'd help me up and tell me "Try again."
Patiently, He molded me like a sculptor molds his clay,
He formed me in His image more and more each day.
As we walked this path called Life, He spoke about His Son,
And about the sacrifice He made so we could be as one.
"I have a job for you," He said. "Come now, have no fear,
I have a message you must share with others far and near.
Tell them all I love them, each and every one,
Tell them of the path we've walked and tell them of my Son.
Tell them I will be with them, and I will hold their hand,

    Speak to them of sweet rewards and of the Promised Land."
    So now I stand before you all with a message of true love,
    Just turn your eyes to Jesus and the Father up above.
    Set your heart upon Him because then you too will see,
    How only the redeeming love of Christ can truly set you free!

Matthew 22:14
"For many are called, but few are chosen."

Prayer:
Father, today I ask You to let me speak boldly of my faith and Your grace. May I never forget to set the example for others around me every day and every moment. Help me to reflect Christ in my actions, attitudes, appearance, and speech. I pray in Jesus' name, amen.

Day 26

"DOWN TIME"

Matthew 11:28
"Come to Me, all you who labor and are heavy laden, and I will give you rest."

Getting "caught up" in our daily lives (jobs, kids, housework, school, etc.) happens so easily. Sometimes we get in such a hurry that we forget to take time for ourselves and for God. I know when I get "caught up" in trying to accomplish all that I need to do in a day without any down time, I get flustered and lose track of all that is important in God's eyes.

Getting overloaded with life's daily issues can be a very slippery spot for a recovering addict. In addiction, our solution was to run from our problems. By this, I mean altering our "state of mind" to separate ourselves from reality.

In recovery, we want to avoid any "hot spots" that may cause us to backslide into old behaviors We need to have a little down time to avoid the build up of emotions that often cause us to feel overwhelmed by life.

Taking time for yourself throughout your busy day for meditation and prayer is a good way to calm any inner turmoil. We all need to connect with God on a daily basis. This will help to carry us through any kind of day we might have.

Psalm 29:11
"The Lord will give strength to His people; The Lord will bless His people with peace."

Exodus 33:14
"My Presence will go with you, and I will give you rest."

God reassures us that He will care for us if we take the time to put our daily lives in His hands. Trying to handle all of what life throws at you alone is impossible. When you go it alone, at some point you will experience failure.

God wants you to trust Him! I Peter 5:7 states, *"Casting all your cares upon Him, for He cares for you."* He wants to be included in your daily life and routine. Relying on Him will help you to avoid those "hot spots" which can cause discouragement and failure. Psalm 46:10 says, *"Be still, and know that I am God..."* Slowing down and being still helps you to be able to hear and plainly see what God would have you do to be successful in all things.

In your down time commune with the Lord, for it's by His strength and wisdom that you will succeed in your walk with Him and in your everyday life.

"YOU"

A beacon in the darkness, a harbor in the storm,
When all seems dark and the waves too high, You protect me from all harm.
Life is full of tests and trials, through which you carry me,
I'd be so lost with out You, Lord, this I finally see.
So in You I put my faith and hope, to You I now belong,
My eyes, O Lord, I turn to you to teach me right from wrong.
When I rise in the morn or rest my head at night,

In You, Lord, I will abide, safely in Your sight.

Isaiah 25:4
"For You have been a strength to the poor, a strength to the needy in his distress, a refuge from the storm, a shade from the heat…"

Prayer:
Lord, I ask that You would help me to remember to rely on You in times of trouble. When things seem too much to bear, I pray the Holy Spirit would draw me back to You and to Your love for me. Help me to learn to be still and know that You are God. Amen

Day 27

"HONESTY"

Psalm 6:16-19:
"These six things the Lord hates, yes, seven are an abomination to Him: A proud look, a lying tongue, hands that shed innocent blood, a heart that devises wicked plans, feet that are swift in running to evil, a false witness who speaks lies, and one who sows discord among brethren."

Boy, this is a hard topic. As a Christian (in recovery or not), this is one subject that has no grey area. One of the Ten Commandments (Exodus 20:1-17) clearly states that we should not lie.

Being honest with yourself and other people is a difficult task. Ephesians 4:29 says, *"Let no corrupt word proceed out of your mouth, but what is good for necessary edification, that it may impart grace to the hearers."* Being honest is a requirement that we must work to achieve on a moment to moment basis – always relying on the Holy Spirit to help us.

In addiction, my favorite lie to myself was that I wasn't hurting anyone but myself by using drugs. In hind sight, how untrue this was. I hurt not only myself but my family, my friends, and countless others along the way. This is just one example of how a lie starts with us and through a domino effect hurts all the others around us.

The Bible tells us the Lord despises liars. Proverbs 12:22 says, *"Lying lips are an abomination to the Lord, but those who deal truthfully are His delight."* We need to learn to be honest in our actions and our words. Always let your yes be yes, and your no be no. Think before you speak and remember God is always listening. Take into consideration how your words affect others and treat them as you would have them treat you.

Ephesians 4:25
"Therefore, putting away lying, let each one of you speak truth to his neighbor, for we are members of one another."

Strive to reflect Christ's character in your own character. This will bring about new traits in you such as honesty, compassion, love, and respect for others and for yourself. Walk before our Lord and be blameless.

1 Peter 3:10-12:
"For 'He who would love life and see good days, let him refrain his tongue from evil, and his lips from speaking deceit. Let him turn away from evil and do good; Let him seek peace and pursue it. For the eyes of the Lord are on the righteous, and His ears are open to their prayers; But the face of the Lord is against those who do evil.'"

EL SHADDAI

  Father God, I thank You for all You are teaching me,
  All the things I never knew like compassion, love, and honesty.
  You alone are God Almighty, the God of Abraham,
  Yesterday, today, and forever, You are the great "I AM".
  You tell us to walk before You blameless and in love,

This will open Heaven's windows and bring blessings from above.

We praise you, Lord Almighty, our Creator, El Shaddai,
We lift our hearts in one accord and worship You on high.

Obedience and healing, faithfulness and love,
Guidance and protection come from the Lord above.
Open up your heart and soul, He will take your hand,
Experience the perfect love of the great "I AM".

Prayer:

Lord, help me today to be hospitable toward all who approach me and to show love to all who cross my path. Teach me to be honest in my actions and my words. Help me to treat others the way I want to be treated. I pray I will not lose sight of what is most important – respect and love for my fellow man. Amen

Day 28

"THANKFULNESS"

Psalm 118:24
"This is the day the Lord has made; We shall rejoice and be glad in it."

On a general basis, we all thank God and praise Him when some big and wonderful thing happens in our lives. What about all the small infinite details that happen on a daily basis? Do you thank Him for the little things? It is so easy to take for granted things like the food we eat, the clothes we wear, the place where we live – just to mention a few.

What about a sunny day, the laughter of a child, or the love of a pet? Have you ever given thanks for any of these things? They may seem like ordinary occurrences to you, but all we love and have that is good, is a gift from God. Each morning that we wake up and start a new day is because He has chosen to grace us with that time. My challenge to you today is to stop for a minute and think of all the gifts He's given you to praise Him for. Do you live in a beautiful home, have children, or have a loving spouse? Do you have a car or a job? Are you in good health?

If you answered yes to even one of these questions, then the Lord has blessed you. Instead of taking everything we know and have for granted, we need to give Him praise and thanks.

Psalm 100:4
"Enter into His gates with thanksgiving, and into His courts with praise. Be thankful to Him and bless His name."

I Thessalonians 5:18

"In everything give thanks; for this is the will of God in Christ Jesus for you."

THANKSGIVING FOR LIFE

Thank you, Jesus, for waking me up and giving me another day,
Thanks for the food I eat and the energy to work and play.
Thank you, Lord, for wellness and protection from above,
But most of all I thank You, Lord, for Your everlasting love.
Your forgiveness and Your mercy are given new each day,
Graciously extended every time we pray.
For this, O Lord, we praise You when we bow our heads in prayer,
We thank You for all the blessings You give that show how much You care.
So I lift my heart in praise and song for all You do each day,
I offer You my heart and soul every time I pray.
Lord, please accept my sacrifice of praise and thanks I give,
O Lord, I need you in my life, I need Your love to live!

Prayer:
Father, help me to praise You for the big and the small things You do for me each day. Let me not overlook the fact that all I have comes from You. You, Lord, are my portion. By Your grace, my cup runs over. Thank You, Father, for Your love, Your forgiveness, and Your generosity. Amen

Psalm 68:19

"Blessed be the Lord, Who daily loads us with benefits, The God of our salvation!"

James 1:17
"Every good gift and every perfect gift is from above, and comes down from the Father of lights, with whom there is no variation or shadow of turning."

Day 29

"WORSHIP"

John 4:23
"But the hour is coming, and now is, when the true worshipers will worship the Father in spirit and truth; for the Father is seeking such to worship Him."

You may wonder what worship has to do with recovery. When you hear the word "worship" you probably think of singing praises to God. However, worship goes so much deeper than that.

How we live our lives moment-to-moment is a form of worship. Ask yourself are you worshiping God with your life or are you worshiping the world? What does your life reflect and where do your priorities lie? When others look at your lifestyle, do they see you as an honest person, a hard worker, a good parent, a faithful loving spouse, and a loyal friend?

Learning to reflect Christ in how we live is a form of worship that can be used as a ministry to others. Matthew 5:16 says, *"Let your light so shine before men, that they may see your good works and glorify your Father in Heaven."*

No part played in serving Christ is considered small. How you live your life may be your ministry. Have you ever considered who's watching you? It may be your spouse, your children, or even your co-workers.

The daily example we set for others may very well be a life changing example. The fruits of your worship are your responsibility. The example you set is up to you. We will all reap what we sow. The fruits of your harvest are your own.

REFLECTING MY CREATOR

Dear Jesus,
Your love I will try to reflect in my love for others.
Your faith I desire to reflect in my faith.
Your perseverance I aspire to show in my perseverance.
Your hope for mankind, I wish to show in my hope for humanity.
Your peace of heart and mind I wish to understand completely.
The joy You have given me I wish to share with others.
Your character I strive to reflect in my character.
Your generosity I wish to reflect in my actions.
Your complete acceptance and understanding of me
   I wish to have for others.
Your laws I wish to have hidden in my heart.
Your statutes I desire to be my statutes.
These are the aspirations of a grateful child to some day be like her Father.

Prayer:
Lord, I pray that I can worship you with all areas of my life. Help me, Lord, to be a light in this world. Let my actions reflect Christ so that my life may be used as a ministry for others-always, drawing them closer to you. Amen

Day 30

"THE LOVE OF MONEY"

1 John 2:15
"Do not love the world or the things in the world."

I remember when I was actively using drugs that money was the driving force that compelled me forward. My sense of what was important was twisted around in my mind and my heart. I felt that to be accepted and successful I had to have money no matter how I got it. I craved worldly acceptance. For me, money was a very real part of my addiction because my need for it drove me deeper into many illegal activities.

I was addicted to the feeling of power and control that hid behind the money I was making. My life was shameless, a hollow shell of drug addiction, homelessness, loneliness, fear, and sickness. I craved some means of control. For me, money was what I used to cover the void of emptiness and helped to make me feel important.

I felt that if I had money my problems would disappear, and I would be accepted by the world despite my character flaws. I was living a lie and that lie permeated every area of my life.

1 Timothy 6:30
"For the love of money is a root of all kinds of evil, for which some have strayed from the faith in their greediness, and pierced themselves through with many sorrows."

I believe this verse describes so many of us. We can all have tendencies to be self concerned, craving worldly things in excessive amounts. We must remember greed is a sin. Nothing we acquire in this life can be taken with us when we die.

Romans 12:2
"And do not be conformed to this world, but be transformed by the renewing of your mind, that you may prove what is that good and acceptable and perfect will of God."

"SAVING GRACE"

Between shattered dreams, a broken heart, and a life in shambles,
The sickness, fear, and sadness is almost too much to handle.
I live in a world of darkness and addiction, evil on every side,
Then I gave my life to Jesus, now I no longer have to hide.
His saving grace surrounds me as He blankets me in His love,
Everyday I'm learning more dependence on the Father up above.
His forgiveness and compassion have truly preserved my soul,
He's brought me to a sacred place--I finally feel whole.
The emptiness inside me is filled up with His love,
His sweet Holy Spirit ascends upon me like a dove.
I praise Your name, sweet Jesus, for all the hope You bring,
I lift my voice in praise, and song to You I sing.
Holy, holy, holy, praise to my Father and my friend,
My confidant, my Savior, I'll worship You until the end.

Prayer:

Father, my prayer today is that all of my goals will be Spirit driven, focusing on God's will and not on what the world portrays as important. Help me not to love the world or the things of the world more than You. I pray that through Your grace and love may I walk in the Spirit focusing on Your heavenly gifts from above. Always remembering that all good things come from You. Amen

Day 31

"GOD'S GUARENTEE"

Romans 8:28
"And we know that all things work together for good to those who love God, to those who are called according to His purpose."

Have you ever felt unsure about your future? During the days of my active addiction, I never knew what to expect from one day to the next. I remember always being worried about where I would sleep, what I would eat, and how I could make my next dollar. I lived in a constant state of fear never knowing what tomorrow would bring, or if there would even be a tomorrow. Many of us live like this on a daily basis, never knowing what to expect from one moment to the next in life. What if I told you it doesn't have to be that way? Wouldn't it be nice to have some sort of guarantee that things would always eventually work out for the best for you? We actually do have that guarantee from the highest authority available.

Proverbs 16:3
"Commit your works to the Lord, and your thoughts will be established."

Jeremiah 29:11
"For I know the thoughts that I think toward you, says the Lord, thoughts of peace and not of evil, to give you a future and a hope."

What a promise! What a guarantee! It's amazing that every difficult situation we face on a daily basis can have a good outcome when placed in God's hands.

Always remember God never breaks a promise and His guarantee never expires. All things work out for good for those who love the Lord; we should never doubt the outcome of any situation we face if we put our trust in God.

Isaiah 41:10
"Fear not, for I am with you; Be not dismayed, for I am your God. I will strengthen you, yes, I will help you, I will hold you with My righteous right hand."

Now I am sure you're wondering could it really be as simple as committing myself to God's expectations? The answer is yes! Abide in Him and He will abide in you and fulfill every promise He has made.

Psalm 40:1-2
"I waited patiently for the Lord; and He inclined to me, and heard my cry. He also brought me up out of a horrible pit, out of miry clay, and set my feet upon the rock, and established my steps."

Victory and success are yours through Christ's sacrifice if you believe in Him and abide by His Word.

"TO THE ONE"

To the Father of all nations in whom my soul abides,
To the One who always loves me, in whom I shall confide.
To the One who never leaves me, who hears me when I call,
To the One who never fails to catch me when I fall.
I want to say how thankful I am for all You do,
For the good and the bad times that You've seen me through.
Your ever constant presence has changed my heart and soul,
Acceptance of Your sacrifice is what finally made me whole.
Your perfect love, joy, and peace have healed my broken heart,
You've taken me from darkness and from You I'll never part.

Prayer:
> Thank You, Lord Jesus, for Your grace, Your patience, and Your unchanging love for me. I commit my life to You, the giver of all good things that You may establish my steps in the direction of fulfillment of the plans You have for me. I ask, Lord, that You would be included in every action and decision that I make today. Guide me by the presence of Your Holy Spirit. I pray in Jesus' name, amen.

Day 32

"WHO IS GOD?"

James 4:8
"Draw near to God and He will draw near to you."

Isaiah 55:6-7
"Seek the Lord while He may be found, Call upon Him while He is near. Let the wicked forsake his way, And the unrighteous man his thoughts; Let him return to the Lord, And He will have mercy on him; And to our God, for He will abundantly pardon."

Some recovery programs teach self-consciousness and awareness or a "higher power" (whoever you determine that to be) and that there are specific steps to follow for recovery. I do believe there are steps that need to be made to aid in our recovery. Two important steps are recognizing our need for help; and, then, deciding to give our will and life over to the only true "higher power", God. To do this, we need an understanding of who God is. So many of us have a preconceived notion of what God is like without ever really knowing Him or even trying to learn what He can truly mean to us on a very personal level. He desires to have a close personal relationship with every one of us. How do you understand God? In your mind, what is He to you?

In order to relate to God and understand how He responds to each of us, you need to know God! You can trust God's Word to show you God and His true nature. You will see there is only one God though He has many names in the original text and language of the Holy Bible. God's names describe His characteristics and attributes. This is important because they also explain His relationship to you! Below is a partial list of God's names and their meanings:

Elohim -- God's name
Jehovah Rophe – I am the Lord your Physician; I am the Lord your Healer
Jehovah Nissi – Our Banner, a banner of love and protection
Jehovah Shammah – The One who is with us everywhere for He is omnipresent
Jehovah Rohi – Our Shepherd who tenderly leads us, loves us, and will keep us safe
Jehovah Jireh – The Lord our Provider
Jehovah Shalom – Our perfect peace
Jehovah M'Kaddesh – The Lord is our righteousness
Jehovah Hoseenu – The Lord our Maker (Creator)
Jehovah Elyon – The Lord Most High
Jehovah Elohay – The Lord my God

As you can see, these names of God are very specific and personal. God wants to reveal Himself to you because He loves you. God refers to Himself in the Bible as "I AM" because in Him you can find all you need. Are you willing to turn your will and life over to Him? Now is the time to reach out; you can truly experience and know God today.

Isaiah 26:3-4
"You will keep him in perfect peace, whose mind is stayed on You, because he trusts in You. Trust in the Lord forever, for in Yah, the Lord, is everlasting strength."

Psalm 23
    "The Lord is my shepherd;
    I shall not want.
    He makes me to lie down in green pastures;
    He leads me beside the still waters.
    He restores my soul;

He leads me in the paths of righteousness
For His name's sake.

Yea, though I walk through the valley of the shadow of death,
I will fear no evil;
For You are with me;
Your rod and Your staff, they comfort me.

You prepare a table before me in the presence of my enemies;
You anoint my head with oil;
My cup runs over.
Surely goodness and mercy shall follow me
All the days of my life;
And I will dwell in the house of the Lord
Forever."

OUR PROVIDER

Elohim is God, full of wisdom, knowledge, and love,
Jehovah Rophe brings us healing from Heaven far above.
Jehovah Nissi brings strength and deliverance by His mighty hand,
From the house of bondage into the "Promised Land".
Jehovah Shammah is always present, tending to every care and need,
Jehovah Rohi means good Shepherd, through the darkness He will lead.
He takes us to still waters; He restores our soul,
Through the valley of death, no evil takes its toll.
Jehovah Hireh expects obedience; Jehovah Shalom brings us peace,
Jehovah M'Kaddesh, our Lord of righteousness; we must listen when He speaks.

Jehovah Hoseenu is our Creator, Lord, and Master of all we see,
Jehovah Elyon is our Lord Most High, Master of you and me.
Jehovah Elohay, my Lord, my God, You deserve all our praise,
May we glorify and honor You all the rest of our days.

Prayer:
Father, I acknowledge You today as my "higher power." Help me, Lord, to look to You for all my needs, wants, and desires. You, Lord, are my all and everything; my Shepherd who restores my soul and directs my path. Let the meditations of my heart focus on You today, Lord, and all that You represent in my life. Amen

Day 33

"WISDOM"

Proverbs 3:7-8
"Do not be wise in your own eyes; fear the Lord and depart from evil. It will be health to your flesh, and strength to your bones."

Learning to live a new life in recovery is not just a journey but a job. Each one of us has a responsibility to seek out our own path. Whatever path you choose will affect every area of your life, your family, your job, and your health. Making wise choices for yourself and your family will become clearer and easier when you learn to seek God first in your life.

How do you gain wisdom for your life? The Bible clearly states that wisdom is from God. James 1:5 says, *"If any of you lacks wisdom, let him ask of God, who gives to all liberally and without reproach, and it will be given to him."* This verse tells us if we don't know what to do, we are to ask God, and God will give us wisdom generously and without disgrace.

Proverbs 2:6-11
"For the Lord gives wisdom; from His mouth comes knowledge and understanding; He stores up sound wisdom for the upright; He is a shield to those who walk uprightly; He guards the paths of justice, and preserves the way of its saints. Then you will understand righteousness and justice, equity and every good path. When wisdom enters your heart, and knowledge is pleasant to your soul, discretion will preserve you; understanding will keep you."

God's wisdom in His Word should be a guideline for every person's life. When we consult God's Word, we learn what His expectations are for us. We learn how to follow His chosen path. It's only then that we find deep peace and lasting contentment. There may still be challenging days, but He will see us through every one.

Proverbs 3:21-26
"My son (child) *let them* (my words) *not depart from your eyes- keep sound wisdom and discretion; so they will be life to your soul and grace to your neck. Then you will walk safely in your way, and your foot will not stumble. When you lie down, you will not be afraid; yes, you will lie down and your sleep will be sweet. Do not be afraid of sudden terror, nor of trouble from the wicked when it comes; for the Lord will be your confidence, and will keep your foot from being caught."*

Remember, we can hide nothing from our Heavenly Father, and, someday, will be held accountable for all the things we do and say. We must learn to control all our actions, attitudes, and speech. How we live our lives and how we affect others is our responsibility. With this in mind, may we be aware of all we do every day.

Proverbs 3:13
"Happy is the man who finds wisdom, and the man who gains understanding."

"A CHILD'S REQUEST"

Heavenly Father, I bow my head and come to You in prayer,
I never have to wait long for You're already there.
Be my light in darkness, in weakness make me strong,
Only You can help me, Lord, teach me right from wrong.

Send me Your Holy Spirit to help my conscience be my guide,
To walk with me and talk with me, ever by my side.
I give You praise and glory, my life, my heart, and soul,
Lord, please be my Master, only You can make me whole.
Even in my darkest hour when things are looking bleak,
I pray to keep my eyes on You and only these words to speak.
Praise You, Lord Almighty, in Heaven far above,
For all the good gifts that You give like joy, and peace, and love.
I put my faith in Your Word, my life in Your hands,
Please carry me through and bring me home to see the Promised Land.

Prayer:
    Lord Jesus, please help me to walk in the wisdom of Your Word daily. I praise You for Your higher consciousness and thank You for being aware of all my needs, wants, and desires. Give me the awareness through Your Holy Spirit to walk in the light at all times, desiring to please You in all things. I pray in Your name, Jesus. Amen

Day 34

"LETTING GO OF THE *WHAT IFS*"

John 15:9
"As the Father loved me, I also have loved you, abide in My love."

Have you ever felt completely alone in the world? Unloved? Unwanted? Not important? Have you ever wondered if anyone would truly love and accept you for who you really are? So many of us have a deep-seated fear that if we expose who we really are on the inside that we may never be loved. This fear leads to the "what ifs." "What if" I expose who I am to any significant person in my life and they reject me! "What if" I get my heart broken? "What if...what if...what if?" The list is endless.

The Bible tells us not to worry about the things of the world or its opinion of us. There is someone who loves you completely and unconditionally despite your faults, flaws, and shortcomings. Did you know you were predestined to be loved, protected, and cared for before you were even born?

Isaiah 43:1
"But now, thus says the Lord, who created you, O Jacob, and He who formed you, O Israel: Fear not, for I have redeemed you; I have called you by name; you are Mine."

God claimed you as His. His unwavering love washes all of the "what ifs" away. Nothing or no one can ever cause God not to love you.

Romans 8:38-39

"For I am persuaded that neither death nor life, nor angels nor principalities nor powers, nor things present nor things to come, nor height nor depth, nor any other created thing shall be able to separate us from the love of God which is in Jesus Christ our Lord."

Lay aside those fears today and open your heart to the perfect love you have always truly desired. It doesn't matter what walk of life you're from or what you've done in the past; God is calling you to come just as you are with an open heart. Come, He will take care of the rest.

"SWEET JESUS"

> Praise You, sweet Jesus, for giving me rest,
> I bask in Your care and sweet tenderness.
> Showers of God's blessings rain down on me,
> Though once I was blind, by grace now I see.
> On the wings of Your angels sent down from above,
> I rest in the presence of Your everlasting love.
> In Your presence, sweet Jesus, I'm finally home,
> No more sadness or sickness or feeling alone.
> Praise You, sweet Jesus, for giving me rest,
> I bask in Your care and sweet tenderness.

Prayer:
> Lord Jesus, I release all of my inhibitions to You. Today, I open my heart despite all the "what ifs" in my mind. I need Your unwavering, everlasting love to wash over me, Lord, and cleanse my spirit. Let today be a new day and a new beginning for me. Amen

Day 35

"FROM WHERE COMES MY HELP"

Proverbs 10:17
"He who keeps instruction is in the way of life, but he who refuses correction goes astray."

In every walk of recovery, three pertinent ideas are always made clear:

> 5. We are addicts and could not manage our own lives.
> 6. Probably no human power could relieve our addiction.
> 7. God could and would if He were sought.

These ideas all point us in the direction of seeking answers outside ourselves and learning redirection through a "higher power." I remember when I first sobered up; all I wished for were simple instructions to follow to be able to cope with all I was experiencing.

The "well" of emotions in my spirit was like a raging river of anger, guilt, self-pity and confusion. It was all very exhausting. Not knowing how to channel these emotions finally drove me to my knees to call on God for help and comfort. When this point is reached by each individual person seeking release, relief is given.

Psalm 121

"I will lift up my eyes to the hills – from whence comes my help? My help comes from the Lord, Who made heaven and earth. He will not allow your foot to be moved; He who keeps you will not slumber. Behold, He who keeps Israel shall neither slumber nor sleep. The Lord is your keeper; The Lord is your shade at your right hand. The sun shall not strike you by day, nor the moon by night. The Lord shall preserve you from all evil; He shall preserve your soul. The Lord shall preserve your going out and your coming in from this time forth, and even forevermore."

Psalm 91:9-12
"Because you have made the Lord, who is my refuge, even the Most High, your dwelling place, no evil shall befall you, nor shall any plague come near your dwelling; For He shall give His angels charge over you, to keep you in all your ways. In their hands they shall bear you up, lest you dash your foot against a stone."

Recovery is not a process that is accomplished alone. My point is that the strength to face anything you are dealing with on the inside or in life can be found when you earnestly seek God's face. Why not reach out and tap into God's supply of strength and help today?

Psalm 46:1
"God is our refuge and strength, a very present help in trouble."

THE FOREST BEYOND THE TREES

> To see the forest beyond the trees,
> Today is still too much for me.
> I turn my eyes, Lord, up to You,
> And focus on Your love so true.
> You build me up each passing day,
> Strengthen me along the way.
> A purpose for me You have I know,
> And You will instruct the way I go.

My pathways of life You must lead,
Filling every want and need.
You've brought me from that place of pain,
And home to be with You again.
Your mercy and forgiveness have cleansed my soul,
I'm starting to heal and to be made whole.
So I lift my hands and my voice to You,
And praise You for Your love so true.

Prayer:
Lord God, I'm thankful that I can place myself under the shelter of Your wings. Thank You, Lord, for Your strength in my weakness. Lord, I pray that You will abide in me, be my rock of safety, and my pillar of strength. Father, You are the Healer of my soul. Amen

Day 36

"SHARING THE BURDEN"

I Thessalonians 5:11
"Therefore comfort each other and edify (build up) *one another, just as you are doing."*

Carrying the cross of our past mistakes, faults, and bad decisions is not a burden we are to bear on our own. In order to move past any harbored feelings we have of guilt, shame, and remorse, we must be willing to lay it all out on the table and get honest with ourselves and others.

Alcoholics Anonymous help addicts like us to recognize and admit our mistakes and improper, destructive choices to God, to ourselves and to others; to be ready and willing to change; and to ask God to help bring about this change in us.

Opening yourself up to another person about what you've done and how you feel can give you a better perspective on where you don't want to go back to and actions you don't want to do again. To get completely honest about past mistakes helps lift the burden of guilt that you have been carrying on your own for so long.

James 5:16
"Confess your trespasses to one another, and pray for another, that you may be healed. The effective, fervent prayer of a righteous man avails much."

Don't be afraid to ask for help—not just from someone you trust, but from God as well. Find an accountability partner; someone who you can share your burdens and your joys with. Hold each other up by praying together and always be honest about your feelings and what you're going through. I can attest to the fact that complete honesty cleanses the soul. Above all, remember, God is always there to help you.

Philippians 1:6
"Being confident of this very thing, that He who has begun a good work in you will complete it until the day of Jesus Christ."

STRONG REALIZATION

Please believe me when I cry out, "I'm sorry for all I've done!"
Thanks to Jesus, my life's not over, it's only just begun.
I've opened up my heart and mind to learn of Jesus' love,
I'm gathering so much strength from Heaven above.
I'm going to break the cycle; just you wait and see,
Through the love and strength of Christ, I'm learning to be me.
I'm moving forward slowly, each day there is great pain,
He's removing all my sorrow, my sickness, and shame.
So with all this mercy I've been shown, I pray to God above,
Father, please protect me and cleanse me with Your love.

Prayer:

Lord, I pray You will lead me to complete honesty with You and myself that I may be healed and set free of the burdens I carry deep within myself. Open my heart, Lord, that I may be forgiven and set free through Your love. Amen

Day 37

"A HEART DEDICATED"

Matthew 22:37
"Jesus said, 'You shall love the Lord your God with all your heart, with all your soul, and with all your mind.'"

What are you truly dedicated to in your life? Is it your job, your hobbies, your children, or your friends? Do any of these things monopolize your life or your free time? If the answer is "yes", then it's time to reprioritize what you consider to be the most important thing in your daily schedule. Always seeking self-satisfaction or constantly trying to please others and meet their needs will never give you the sense of fulfillment you crave in your soul. There is a desire deep within each of us to find our purpose and pour our whole heart and soul into that one thing. This desire comes from God. In order to discover the purpose He created you for, you must prioritize your daily life, putting Him above everything else. The Bible says in Matthew 22:37 to love the Lord your God with <u>all</u> your heart, soul, and mind—that means with everything you have! If we just spent a portion of the time with our Savior that we do at work, or with our families, or even with our friends, our lives would change drastically.

We were created for a special part in God's intricate plan and each one of us has a specific calling (direction/job) that God wants us to fulfill.

My challenge to you, today, is to reprioritize your schedule. Try spending ten extra minutes a day in prayer or reading your Bible. Ask God to clarify His expectations of you. Trust Him to open the doors He wants you to walk through and close the ones He doesn't.

PLEASING YOU

Only pleasing You, Lord is truly my life's goal,
To You, I open my heart and mind and dedicate my soul.
An indwelling of Your Spirit will surely renew my mind,
Washing away the sins of the past and leaving them all behind.
To refresh and renew the inner man is the promise You made to me,
By opening up my life to You, You promised to set me free.
I give You all my burdens, my sorrows, and my loss,
As my Father, You smile and say, "Leave them at the cross.
I give you love and healing and forgiveness through My Son,
Open up your heart to Me, and we shall be as one."

John 14:23
"Jesus answered and said to him, 'If anyone loves me, he will keep My word; and My Father will love him, and We will come to him and make Our home with him.'"

Isaiah 26:3
"You will keep him in perfect peace, whose mind is stayed on You, because he trusts in You."

Prayer:

Heavenly Father, I ask You, today, to clarify Your expectations of me. Open the doors You would have me walk through Lord. As I put my faith in Your Word, instruct me in the pathway of my life. I'm leaving it in Your hands to guide me. Use me as a vessel for Your will, Lord, not my own. Amen

Day 38

"THE BIBLE OUR FOUNDATION"

I Thessalonians 5:9
"But let us who are of the day be sober, putting on the breastplate of faith and love, and as a helmet the hope of salvation."

Today I want to discuss why using God's Word to grow in recovery from addiction is so important.

2 Timothy 3:16-17
"All Scripture is given by inspiration of God, and is profitable from doctrine, for reproof, for correction, for instruction in righteousness, that the man of God may be complete, thoroughly equipped for every good work."

Studying God's Word will result in several important developments:

> 8. A solid foundation in the basic doctrines of the Bible. This is very important because what we believe affects our behavior and the course of our lives.
> 9. Using reproof from Scripture as a guide for our behavior and through the conviction of the Holy Spirit, this lets God shape our lives while helping us to conform to the image of Christ.
> 10. Correction in the direction of our lives. God's Word gives us a new perspective for living. Through His Word, God speaks the positive aspects of correction. This way we are turned from sin toward a new lifestyle of pleasing God and being fruitful.

11. Instruction in righteousness. Not only does God censor our behavior and gives us a new direction, He promises to instruct us. Psalm 32:8 says, *"I will instruct and teach you in the way you should go; I will guide you with my eye."*
12. Mature and equip for service. As we apply God's Word, He leads us into appropriate behaviors and a new lifestyle by which we can live a life of satisfactory measures in purity, honesty, humility, and having respect for ourselves and others. Joshua 1:8 says, *"This book of the Law shall not depart from your mouth, but you shall meditate in it day and night, that you may observe to do according to all that is written in it. For then you will make your way prosperous, and then you will have good success."*

GRATEFUL PRAISE

Thank You, Lord, for truly giving me,
Such a wonderful salvation so rich and free.
Your gracious mercy reigns down from above,
On all who believe in Your everlasting love.
Your patience and understanding You've given to all,
If only upon Your name we will call.
Father, I praise You for letting me see
You in all Your glorious majesty.
You've given me a purpose, a life, and a name,
A daughter and servant, I finally became.
A vessel of Your will, I'm honored to be,
As living sacrifice, I offer myself to Thee.
Here I am, sweet Savior, teach me Your ways,
May I be an example the rest of my days.

Prayer:
> Father, I pray that You would give me an understanding of Your Word and its importance in my life to teach and guide me. Open my eyes and ears that I may hear and comprehend all that You are speaking to me. Instruct the pathways of my life, Lord, that I may be a success in Your eyes. Amen

Day 39

"TOOLS OF THE TRADE"

Proverbs 16:20
"He who heeds the word wisely will find good, and whoever trusts in the Lord, happy is he."

This is just a short review of what we've covered so far regarding recovery based on biblical views. We must realize the most important tool that we use to succeed will always be the Word of God. God's Word is all powerful; it represents true knowledge, all wisdom, and pure truth. God's Word gives us direction and instruction on every expectation of the Father. God promises victory through His Word when we stand in faith and trust in Him.

GOD IS INFALLABLE:
Psalm 18:30
"As for God, His way is perfect; The word of the Lord is proven; He is a shield to all who trust in Him."

Proverbs 30:5
"Every word of God is pure; He is a shield to those who put their trust in Him."

GOD IS MERCIFUL:
Proverbs 28:13
"He who covers his sins will not prosper, but whoever confesses and forsakes them will have mercy."

GOD IS AVAILABLE AND PERSONAL:
Psalm 91:14-16

"Because he has set his love upon Me, therefore I will deliver him; I will set him on high because he has known My name. He shall call upon Me and I will answer him; I will be with him in trouble; I will deliver him and honor him. With long life I will satisfy and show him My salvation."

GOD IS PROTECTIVE:
Psalm 91:10
"No evil shall befall you, nor shall any plague come near your dwelling."

Proverbs 3:26
"For the Lord will be your confidence, and will keep your foot from being caught."

GOD IS WISE:
Proverbs 3:5-6
"Trust in the Lord with all your heart, and lean not on your own understanding; In all your ways acknowledge Him, and He shall direct your paths."

GOD IS FORGIVING:
John 3:16-17
"For God so loved the world that He gave His only begotten Son, that whoever believes in Him should not perish but have everlasting life. For God did not send His Son into the world to condemn the world, but that the world through Him might be saved."

GOD IS FAITHFUL AND CARING:
Psalm 103:2-5
"Bless the Lord, O my soul, and forget not all His benefits: Who forgives all your iniquities, Who heals all your diseases, Who redeems your life from destruction, Who crowns you with loving kindness and tender mercies: Who satisfies your mouth with good things, so that your youth is renewed like the eagle's."

Now after reading just these few passages, I hope you have a true understanding of the encompassing love of God and the victory we hold through Christ by our faith in Him and His Word. He, Himself, will arm us with all we need to fight the battle of life and addiction, always carrying us by His strength to success.

IN BONDAGE NO MORE

My faith lives in the sacrifice that You've made for me,
Through God's grace and salvation, I finally know I'm free.
I no longer live in bondage to death or to sin,
I can take a stand, my live can now begin.
I no longer listen to the father of lies —
Satan can't have me, no matter how he tries!
Saved by Christ's mercy I battle no more,
I don't have to fight because He's won the war.
Through His death and resurrection, the price has been paid,
The gavel has fallen, the decisions have been made.
I belong to the Father, through the death of His Son,
My debt has been paid, we now are one.
Sweet peace and contentment are finally mine,
True joy and love, I finally did find.
Give your heart to Jesus and you too will see,
You've been forgiven and forever set free.

Prayer:

Lord Jesus, I pray that You would open my heart to the truth found in Your Word concerning me. Give me the eyes to see and the ears to hear you, O Lord. I pray that through Your promises my faith would grow. Hear the voice of my supplications, O Lord, that I may draw closer to You and abide under the shelter of Your wings. Amen

Day 40

"WALKING IN THE SPIRIT"

Galatians 5:16
"...Walk in the Spirit, and you will not fulfill the lust of the flesh."

As you now contemplate God's will for your life, know this: His deepest desire is for you to live a spirit-filled life and to always look to Him for all things. He tells us directly in His Word that He will always be with us no matter what we're facing.

Genesis 28:15
"Behold, I am with you and will keep you wherever you go..."

Looking back at some of the places I've been and the situations I put myself in, I know that this is the truth. If Jesus had not been with me, I would not be here today.

In order to live a life of purpose and reap God's benefits, we must take certain steps found in Scripture:

PURITY:
Colossians 3:5
"Therefore put to death ...fornication, uncleanness, passion, evil desire, and covetousness, which is idolatry."

HUMILITY AND RESPECT:
Philippians 2:3
"Let nothing be done through selfish ambition or conceit, but in lowliness of mind let each esteem others better than himself.

FORGIVENESS:
Colossians 3:13
"...bearing with one another, forgiving one another, if anyone has a complaint against another; even as Christ forgave you, so you also must do."

HONESTY:
Leviticus 19:11
"You shall not steal, nor deal falsely, nor to lie to one another."

LOVE:
Leviticus 19:18
"You shall not take vengeance, nor bear any grudge...but you shall love your neighbor as yourself: I am the Lord."

When we walk in these statutes, the Lord gives us three things:

13. Victory: Galatians 5:16 states, "*Walk in the Spirit and you will not fulfill the lust of the flesh.*" God gives us the strength to change our behaviors, attitudes, and our lives – we can't do this alone!
14. Power: James 4:7 states, "*Therefore submit to God. Resist the devil and he will flee from you.*" The Holy Spirit gives us the power to resist and rebuke the devil in Jesus' name.
15. Quality of life: Galatians 5:22-23 states, "*But the fruit of the Spirit is love, joy, peace, long suffering, kindness, goodness, faithfulness, gentleness and self-control. Against such there is no law.*" When the Spirit controls our lives, He will produce these things in us.

Remember, each of us can have victory over any and all worldly lusts, desires, and habits. All it takes is choosing to believe in Jesus Christ as our Savior When we ask Christ into our hearts, He brings the indwelling of the Holy Spirit into our lives. Through this indwelling of God's Spirit, He teaches us good from bad, right from wrong, and gives us the strength to overcome the wiles of the devil. In the words of Christ Himself, He tells us we must choose if we will serve God, or will we serve Satan and be conformed to the world? Who will you choose to serve?

ONLY YOU

Only you can change my life, O Lord,
Only You take away burdens and strife, O Lord.
You've opened my eyes and I finally see,
It is You that I need to truly be free.
Free in my heart, free in my mind,
Peace and contentment, I will finally find.
You've lifted me up and set me apart,
You've told me to follow You with all of my heart.
So I will seek guidance from Heaven above,
I will pray for mercy, forgiveness, and love.
Holy Spirit, please guide me in what I should do,
To walk with the Father in His love so true.
Help me, O Lord, to start each day fresh,
To walk in the Spirit and not in the flesh.
Uphold me in weakness and help me be strong,
May Your Spirit guide me to choose right from wrong.
Guide me and keep me, be a light for my path,
Give me Your joy and teach me to laugh.
In your presence, sweet Jesus, I desire to be,
To worship and serve you for eternity.

Prayer:
Lord, I place myself in your hands. From this day forward, I ask that You would guide me, instruct me, protect me, heal me, and forgive me when I stumble. Lord, I pray that You would fill me with Your strength and power for I know that it is only through You that I will find purpose in my life. Let me not be misled by the world but instead led by the Lover of my soul into the light of eternity. Amen

Footprints
by Author Unknown

One night a man had a dream. He dreamed he was walking along the beach with the Lord. Across the sky flashed scenes from his life. For each scene, he noticed two sets of footprints in the sand; one belonged to him, and the other to the Lord.

When the last scene of his life flashed before him, he looked back at the footprints in the sand. He noticed that many times along the path of his life there was only one set of footprints. He also noticed that it happened at the very lowest and saddest times of his life.

This really bothered him and he questioned the Lord about it. "Lord, you said that once I decided to follow you, you'd walk with me all the way. But I have noticed that during the most troublesome times in my life, there is only one set of footprints. I don't understand why when I needed you most you would leave me."

The Lord replied, "My precious, precious child, I love you and I would never leave you. During your times of trial and suffering, when you see only one set of footprints, it was then that I carried you."

Matthew 25:31-40

"When the Son of Man comes in His glory, and all the holy angels with Him, then He will sit on the throne of His glory. All the nations will be gathered before Him, and He will separate them one from another, as a shepherd divides his sheep from the goats. And He will set the sheep on His right hand, but the goats on the left. Then the King will say to those on His right hand, 'Come, you blessed of My Father, inherit the kingdom prepared for you from the foundation of the world: for I was hungry and you gave Me food; I was thirsty and you gave Me drink; I was a stranger and you took Me in; I was naked and you clothed me; I was sick and you visited Me; I was in prison and you came to Me.' Then the righteous will answer Him, saying, 'Lord, when did we see You hungry and feed You, or thirsty and give You drink? When did we see you a stranger and take You in, or naked and clothe You? Or when did we see You sick, or in prison, and come to You?' And the King will answer and say to them, 'Assuredly, I say to you, inasmuch as you did it to one of the least of these My brethren, you did it to Me.'"

Serenity Prayer
by Reinhold Niebuhr*

God, grant me the serenity to accept the things I cannot change,
Courage to change the things I can, and the wisdom to know the difference.

Living one day at a time; enjoying one moment at a time;
Accepting hardship as the pathway to peace.

Taking, as He did, this sinful world as it is, not as I would have it;
Trusting that He will make all things right if I surrender to His will;
That I may be reasonably happy in this life,
And supremely happy with Him forever in the next. Amen

Reinhold Niebuhr is generally credited with writing the "Serenity Prayer".
(June 21, 1892 – June 1, 1971)

Closing Thoughts

I hope that reading my book has opened new chapters of choice in your life. The ultimate question truly is, "Whom will you serve?" I just want to give glory to God for directing the path of my life in the right direction and giving me hope, joy, and a reason for living. There will never be enough words to express my love and gratitude for His sacrifice, His faithfulness, and His long suffering patience to me. I pray the love of Christ will touch your heart and renew your life as it has mine. May God bless and keep you. May His love enfold your life in the protection of His mighty mercy and grace.

Made in United States
Troutdale, OR
08/21/2024

22221513R00080